Awakening To

Lama Migmar Tseten

Mangalamkosha Publications
PO Box 391042
Cambridge, MA 02139 USA
www.lamamigmar.net

ISBN 978-1497426696

Awakening To The Noble Truth

Lama Migmar Tseten

Table Of Contents

Preface

These teachings on the Four Noble Truths were conducted over the course of several months by Khenpo Lama Migmar at the Sakya Institute in Cambridge, MA. The classes were then transcribed and adapted to book form.

In an effort to promote the accessibility of these teachings, we have chosen to leave the transcriptions much as they were. For this reason the book remains conversational in nature and the editing less refined than a scholarly text would require.

Whether you are new to Buddhism or a long time practitioner, we hope that these pages deepen your understanding of the Four Noble Truths and inspire your practice. May all sentient beings everywhere be free from suffering.

Mangalamkosha Publications
Cambridge, MA
May 2014

Chapter One
The First Noble Truth - Suffering

The Four Noble Truths are regarded as the central teaching of the Buddhist tradition and provide the framework upon which all other Buddhist philosophy and meditation are based. Although we may already be familiar with this core doctrine, by repeatedly studying the Four Noble Truths and their sixteen corresponding aspects, our realizations on the spiritual path can become more transformative and profound.

These noble truths are as follows: the truth of suffering, the truth of the origin of suffering, the truth of the cessation of suffering, and the truth of the path leading to the cessation of this suffering.

These four truths are based on the realizations of the prince Siddhartha, who would later reach enlightenment to become the Buddha Shakyamuni. It is said that the Buddha's very first teachings after attaining enlightenment, were these teachings on the Four Noble Truths.

Prince Siddhartha's early life in India was one of great wealth and privilege, where he was given every luxury imaginable. But he soon realized that none of these comforts were bringing him true happiness, and he began to venture outside the palace walls.

On these early trips, the young prince was first exposed to the sufferings of impermanence. As he toured the town he saw the sick, the aging, and the dying people in the streets. He recognized that, in spite of all of the comforts one may possess, no one can avoid the sufferings of sickness, old age, and death.

As he continued to venture from the palace, Prince Siddhartha also saw a meditator and was introduced to the idea of a spiritual life. This was the moment in which he saw that there was another way to live.

At this point he abandoned his life as a prince and renounced the kingdom. He dedicated his life to spiritual practice and eventually came to the profound realization of enlightenment. Through this awakening he came to recognize the Four Noble Truths, including the Noble Eightfold Path, which outlines the essence of Buddhist practice and provides eight practical instructions that lead to the cessation of all suffering.

These eight interconnected factors are to be developed simultaneously in our lives, and they instruct us on the following ways to live: right view, right intention, right speech, right action, right livelihood, right effort, right mindfulness and right concentration.

It is essential in our perfection of the practice that we not only comprehend these Four Noble Truths intellectually but that we integrate this wisdom into our meditation and into every aspect of our lives.

Shamatha Meditation

The most effective method to begin cultivating some realization of the First Noble Truth, the noble truth of suffering, is to begin to practice shamatha meditation. Through gradually training our minds to remain focused on one object of meditation for a period of time, we start to familiarize ourselves with the underlying thought patterns and afflictive emotions which cause so much restlessness and suffering in our lives.

To those who have not done any meditation, shamatha practice may at first sound very easy or relaxing. We are instructed to focus our attention on one single object, most often a blue flower or our breath.

As we begin this practice, we discover it is actually very challenging to sit still. The mind is constantly distracted with racing thoughts and conflicting emotions. What we believed might be relaxing is actually very difficult at first! Our physical bodies are filled with discomfort and our minds suddenly seem even more restless and distracted than ever before. This early stage is crucial to our recognition of the nature of suffering. Through observing this discomfort, we begin to see that we are always running away from these feelings. When we cease to distract ourselves with worldly activities, we notice that there is tremendous suffering just beneath the surface of even a seemingly happy or privileged life.

If we persevere with our shamatha practice for a period of time, we will begin to gain some experience. There are five different levels of realization in shamatha meditation which are compared to different states of water, ranging from the first stage in which the mind is a waterfall of rushing thoughts, to the fifth stage in which the mind has attained a state like that of an ocean without waves.

At this fifth level of shamatha meditation, we have reached a stage of very good attention without much distraction and disturbance. When we experience this fifth level of concentration, we will observe that our minds have become very clear and mindful. Now the shamatha meditation can become the base on which we cultivate more insight meditation.

With that insight we will begin to see something we have never seen before. We will begin to recognize that what we have believed was real in the past is not actually true. Perhaps the Four Noble Truths are called "noble truths" because they help us to move beyond our conditioning towards a more accurate view of the reality of our human existence.

Through very deep insight during meditation, our old view of the nature of our lives begins to fall apart. This can be very frightening without proper training and guidance because all of our former conceptions of reality are shattered. Our way of looking at life is completely transformed, and we come to understand that our previous ways of seeing were all based on misperceptions.

Our old view of life was based on lies, on relativity, on false conditioning. With the cultivation of shamatha and insight meditations, we come to deeply understand the profound meaning of the Four Noble Truths, and we are introduced to the path that can lead us beyond the confines of our suffering.

We recognize these noble truths when we first begin to see things with a very clear mind and without any emotions. This perceptual change affects not only how we see ourselves but how we view all other objects. For the first time we realize that what we have seen and experienced in the past is mostly due to our inner emotional conditions. We understand that we have falsely projected many things onto outer objects as well as onto our own idea of ourselves.

As our insight deepens, all these projections start to dissolve. This false reality we have constructed actually begins to shatter. As we progress from shamatha meditation to the practice of insight meditation, our realizations will counteract many of the misconceptions we have projected onto different objects.

Four Aspects of The First Noble Truth of Suffering:
Impermanence, Suffering, Insubstantiality, and Emptiness

Each of the Four Noble Truths has four different aspects, and we will explore these sixteen aspects more thoroughly through the course of these teachings. Understanding these aspects is based on our insight and on the clarity of each of our minds. As our vision grows purer, these aspects become more apparent.

Impermanence

The first aspect of the First Noble Truth is the aspect of impermanence. Impermanence is the understanding that whatever is created due to causes and conditions is subject to decay. Everything is changing, and nothing can remain forever.

In order to understand our own impermanence, we must first examine what we are made of. According to Buddhist philosophy we consist of "five aggregates" which are the foundation of our current experience. These five aggregates are as follows: the physical body and matter, feelings, ideations, formations (which includes all of the other emotions), and the mind and mental consciousness. These are the five aggregates that are the basis of all of our physical and mental experiences.

Normally in our lives, we possess a very strong attachment to the five aggregates. Due to our strong attachment we have many misconceptions. Although subconsciously at some level we know that we are constantly changing and that we will eventually grow old and die, due to our very strong attachment to our bodies, we remain in denial about our own impermanence.

Although intellectually we understand that whatever is born has to decay, due to our attachments we become ignorant of this reality in our daily lives. No one wants to get older. No one wants to get sick. No one wants to experience the death of a loved one. Due to this fear we create a strong sense of denial around impermanence.

There is a real conflict between our attachment to these five aggregates and the truth of impermanence. No matter how much attachment we may have to our physical bodies, they are constantly changing every moment. Our feelings are changing. Our ideas are changing. Our emotional states are changing. Our consciousness is constantly shifting. All of these aggregates are impermanent and they are continuously in a state of flux.

So the truth of impermanence and change versus our attachment to the five aggregates, creates an underlying conflict in our lives. As a consequence, whenever we are confronted with the truth of impermanence we experience tremendous pain and suffering.

The Three Kinds Of Suffering

The second aspect of the First Noble Truth is suffering itself. There are three main types of suffering. First, we have the *suffering of suffering*, which includes all the physical illnesses and discomforts. Sickness is called the suffering of suffering because it is adding physical or emotional pain to our underlying state of suffering.

The second type of suffering is the *suffering of change*. The source of this suffering is often very surprising to people. This suffering actually stems from all of our pleasurable experiences and all of our conditional states of happiness.

Nothing in this life can stay the same, but we often remain ignorant of this impermanence. When you fall in love with someone, you expect that blissful state of happiness to be permanent. When the relationship begins to change, when you begin to see your partner's flaws and you start to argue, you experience much suffering.

When you first have a child you are so excited, and you feel that your baby is lovely and has made your life complete. Then when the child gets older and begins to separate from you and becomes a difficult teenager, the child can become a source of pain. You miss that baby, and you wish you could go back to that happy time in your family.

What we fail to see is that our suffering is actually rooted in that original happiness. All of these delightful experiences are actually the suffering of change because they become the causes and conditions for future pain and suffering. Since anything good will inevitably change, then our greatest pleasure is already sowing the seeds of loss and disappointment.

The third type of suffering is the *suffering of conditioned nature*. We are all going to grow old and die. Nothing in this life can stay the same. Everything will decay and change over time.

This third form of suffering is actually the basis for both the suffering of suffering and the suffering of change. The suffering of conditioned nature is referring to conception and to the very beginning of the five aggregates within a person. You could say that from the very moment that we are conceived, we are already beginning to die. Everything in this life is conditioned, and this impermanence is at the root of all our suffering.

These three kinds of suffering become much more intensified when our emotions are involved. If we have no meditation experience, then the changing aspects of our lives will create many difficult feelings for us.

So we see that all three kinds of suffering are magnified because they are related to the destructive emotions. The suffering of suffering is related to the destructive emotion of anger. The suffering of change is related to emotions of desire and attachment. And the suffering of conditioned nature is based on our ignorance.

Suffering is constant in our lives because every moment is filled with change and impermanence. Even when things are going well, we have an underlying fear of our inevitable death. On a deep level we are still trying to distract ourselves from the truth of our conditioned existence.

In our lives we are constantly striving for happiness and pleasure. Everything we do in our lives is motivated by our desire for pleasure and comfort. We are completely driven by our attachments, and we are ignoring the suffering nature of our lives. This ignorance to the causes of suffering and this effort to cling to our pleasurable experiences creates tremendous conflict in us.

When we practice insight meditation we begin to see deeper and deeper into the nature of our lives. We recognize the truth of change and impermanence. This seeing helps us begin accepting the reality of our lives.

This acceptance happens when we truly understand our attachment as the cause of our emotional pain. We don't want to die, but the nature of life is impermanence. Through meditation, when we begin to accept the truth of suffering and its causes, the conflict at the very core of our existence begins to dissolve.

Only through insight meditation, when our minds are clearer, and we are free from all the destructive emotions, will we see impermanence more clearly. We will begin to see the suffering nature of conditioned existence.

When we can observe that every moment everything is changing, we can stop clinging to our lives. We can stop living in fear of our own deaths. We can begin to move beyond our ignorance to see the noble truth of suffering.

Insubstantiality and the Five Aggregates

The third aspect of the First Noble Truth is insubstantiality. Another way for us to understand the truth of suffering is for us to integrate it into our five aggregates. As we have discussed, each person has the five aggregates of form, feeling, ideation, formation, and consciousness. Through developing stronger insight meditation, we come to know the characteristics of all of these aggregates.

The first aggregate of form or matter is, of course, what our material body consists of. While we are alive we have this physical component. This is the aggregate of matter.

Once we know the nature of our physical bodies, we will also understand the nature of other people's bodies. Their bodies are impermanent just like ours. This observation will help us to understand how all other material things outside of our bodies are also impermanent.

Buddha said in the Sūtra that as our insight meditation deepens, not only do we see impermanence in ourselves, but we can begin to see impermanence in all living beings. We can also begin to see impermanence in all material things. By realizing the changing nature of our own bodies, we can learn to recognize this impermanence in all sentient beings and all physical matter.

By nature, all physical matter is composed of material atoms. These atoms are comprised of the four basic elements of earth, water, fire, and air. If we look deeper into these atoms, then all material things begin to lose their identification. At the atomic level, what reference do we have with which to identify an object? At the level of the atom we discover the insubstantiality of all objects.

Generally in our lives, we don't break things down to the atomic level, and instead we assign an identity or label to each object in the material world. Then, based on its usefulness to us, we get attached. It is one thing to enjoy something and to let it go. But if we get emotionally attached to it and then something happens to that object, we will experience so much suffering of change.

The second aggregate is that of feeling. Based on the recognition of our own feelings, we can comprehend that other beings have feelings. If we look closely at feelings, whether they are pleasure or pain, happiness or unhappiness, even neutral feelings, they are all a form of suffering. This is because feelings are based on the five aggregates, and the five aggregates are defiled.

Even a neutral feeling is a form of suffering. Neutral feelings are a result of our underlying ignorance. This ignorance is the basis of all the suffering of suffering and the suffering of change.

Through contemplation we can recognize the insubstantiality of feelings. If we look closely, can we find any lasting feeling? Any substantial or permanent feeling state? The same principles apply to the rest of the five aggregates, of ideations, formations, and consciousness. They are all insubstantial.

See, insubstantiality is not limited only to material things. Consciousness and emotions are not material. But what is the mind? Even with strong insight, if we look into the mind, we cannot actually find the mind! The mind loses its own identification.

Emptiness

The fourth aspect of the First Noble Truth is emptiness. When we look deeper and deeper into any of the five aggregates, we cannot find lasting evidence of them. They are insubstantial. As our meditation deepens, we begin to go beyond all concepts, beyond all identification of objects, to discover the emptiness nature.

Right now in our lives, we have lots of attachment to objects. Whenever something happens to those objects of attachment, we experience pain and suffering. This is due to the fact that we have believed that these objects are real and substantial. It is very difficult for us to see the emptiness nature without meditation experience.

An understanding of impermanence can only arise from deep insight meditation experience. Through reflection, we see the impermanent and empty nature of all things. This realization counteracts our misconceptions of reality. We even come to accept and eventually embrace the inevitability of our own death.

By learning to view even our happy feelings as a cause of suffering, we can counteract the misconception that life should always be pleasurable. As long as we are expecting life to be pleasurable, we will constantly be disappointed and experience pain instead. As long as we have emotional attachment to objects, thinking that they are real, we will experience much pain and sadness when we lose them.

To counteract these attachments, we need to develop a profound understanding of the insubstantiality and emptiness nature of those objects, emotions, thoughts, and even of the mind itself. Reflecting and meditating on each aspect of the Four Noble Truths helps to counteract all our misconceptions about reality.

In our lives we cling to the idea of a "self." Most of what we do in our lives is based on "self-cherishing" because we believe that the self and ego truly exist. As we have discussed, the objects of all of our attachments are rooted in the five aggregates. This self-cherishing is based on our bodies, our feelings, our ideas, our habitual patterns, and our consciousness.

When we look deeper, we discover there is no substance to what we thought was existing. That's why emptiness, the fourth aspect of the First Noble Truth, includes not only the emptiness nature of ourselves, but of other objects as well. They are all empty. The insubstantiality and emptiness aspects help us to overcome the misconception of self, which is based on our five aggregates.

These aspects also help us to overcome all our ideas of ownership based on our sense of self. Concepts like "my" are based on the idea of the phenomenal self arising from the five aggregates. These notions of "my house" or "my car" are all arising from misconceptions related to the five aggregates. We each have attachment to ourselves and to the whole universe. It is very important to understand the aspects of insubstantiality and emptiness in order to counteract these attachments.

We can study the Four Noble Truths and gain some intellectual understanding. But only when it becomes true experience through deep insight meditation, will it become a Noble Truth. Through meditation we learn to see these four aspects: impermanence, suffering, insubstantiality, and emptiness; in all five aggregates of ourselves, other beings, and all other things in the conditioned world.

When we see in this way, then we are seeing the First Noble Truth because we are seeing right through our misconceptions. We are no longer clouded by our desires. We are no longer seeing reality through anger or ignorance.

At this level, we have gone beyond all three afflictive emotions of attachment, anger, and ignorance. We have stopped viewing the world through the lens of these emotions, and we have stopped relating to ourselves and those around us with desire, anger, or indifference. Now we are gaining some wisdom, some equanimity in our experience.

The Noble Truth or insight, means seeing with wisdom; seeing with equanimity that is free from all destructive emotions. We no longer have the inner conditions with which we falsely project our emotions onto an object. The way we see reality will be very different.

That's why it is called a "Noble Truth." When we see beyond our delusions, we will realize for the first time that what we saw before was actually defiled. We will realize that our old way of seeing was tainted. It was all based on misconceptions.

The way yogis see, and the way we see now, are two completely different experiences of reality! What we see is based on ignoble perceptions. If we have ignorance, then we will have all the other emotions. Then everything we see will be affected by those other emotions.

But when we can see through our delusions to the Noble Truth, we recognize that the nature of all our feelings was suffering. Only nirvāṇa is unconditioned, and is beyond death. Nirvāṇa is the cessation of feelings that were rooted in the ego. All feelings, even neutral feelings, are rooted in the ego. The seed of these feelings is poisonous. Whatever grows from such a seed is always poisonous.

But through practice, as we recognize the wisdom of the Four Noble Truths, we will see that there is an entirely new way to experience our lives.

Q & A

Q: Lama could you discuss a little more about "the suffering of conditions?"

A: We can understand the suffering of conditions in a few different ways. If we want to understand it from an emotional point of view, then suffering of conditioned nature is based on ignorance. Ignorance is the first link of the twelve interdependent links. This is the basic ignorance of not knowing ourselves and not seeing the nature of the self and ego. Out of that ignorance we have desire. If our desires are not fulfilled, we have anger. These are the three destructive emotions we call the "three poisons."

Because we have ignorance then we have all the other interdependent links. Due to ignorance, we are conceived. Because we are conceived, we are born. Our ignorance generates so many feelings related with our bodies. Because we were conceived, then we have this human form and all the five aggregates. Every moment we are changing, with the biggest change being death.

If we look closely, we realize that every moment that we are alive we are also dying. Physically we are changing. Mentally we are changing. Our feelings are changing. Physically, even our cells are changing every moment. Our cells are moving towards that big change which we call death.

Conditioned nature is as follows: Because of ignorance we are conceived; due to this conception we are subject to decay, change, sickness, and death. This is our conditioned nature. The conditioned nature is like the base. On that base, when we experience sickness or

Awakening To The Noble Truth

pain, then we call it the suffering of suffering. Or when there's happiness and pleasure, that's actually the suffering of change, since we know that it will not last.

So the suffering of suffering is, in some sense, a result of us not wanting to feel pain. The suffering of change is a result of us wanting our pleasurable experiences to remain constant.

When we have pain we may get angry. Anger is often the first response. When we experience happiness, it often increases our desire. And as we have discussed, ignorance is the cause of our underlying base of the suffering of conditioned existence. So we can see how these three emotions increase the three types of suffering. Anger and desire arise because we are born with that basic ignorance. Ignorance is the main cause of suffering. So that is the conditioned nature of suffering.

Often, however, we don't see the truth of this underlying suffering of conditioned nature. We experience the suffering of suffering because sickness and injury are very painful and tangible. We are also able to acknowledge the suffering of change because we experience the loss of pleasure and happiness.

But many times it is harder for us to accept the conditioned nature as suffering because it has a quality of being a bit of a neutral experience. It's not as apparent as painful or pleasurable experiences are. It is more subtle. But that neutral feeling is based on ignorance. That's why even that neutrality, based on ignorance, is a form of suffering because that is the cause of all of the other destructive emotions.

24

Q: So the first two kinds of suffering are actually based on the third type of suffering, but they are more specific?

A: Yes

Q: Lama, would you please talk a little more about the aggregate of formation?

A: The aggregate of formation is actually a bit complex because it includes all Buddhist psychological studies. All mental activities are included, and all emotions are included. Formation, if we study deeply, is described in two Abhidharma texts. According to the Abhidharma Kosha there are forty-six mental activities and fourteen non-mental formations that are included in the aggregate of formation. Then there's another Abhidharma text called the Abhidharma Samuccaya. This text includes fifty-one mental and emotional activities within the aggregate of formation.

It's called "formation" because these mental activities are the formation of karma. If we study each mental activity, we learn that some of those mental activities are positive, some are negative, and some are neutral. We can define all the mental activities according to these three categories.

Even the second aggregate of feeling and the third aggregate of ideation are really part of the fourth aggregate of formation. Feeling and ideation have very critical roles in our lives, which is why Buddha emphasized them. But they are also part of the aggregate of formation.

Formation includes all of the emotions and mental activities which are other than mind. So faith, diligence, jealousy, ignorance – all of the emotions are included in formation. So this is a huge subject!

Mind is like a food cooked with many different spices. Mind has many ingredients. Just because we taste the stronger spice, doesn't mean there are no other spices. So when we get angry, that anger overtakes all the other emotions. That doesn't mean there's no longer ignorance or desire or jealousy. Those feelings are still there, but whatever the strongest emotion is takes over.

So that's why, with formation, we study all those things that obscure the nature of the mind. We learn how many emotions there are in the mind. The mind is complex. All these emotions are in the mind, but we feel and we experience only those which are very active. This does not mean that the sleeping emotions aren't still present.

So if we want to study this in depth, we can read the Abhidharma Kosha. We can also study the Abhidharma Samuccaya. These are the two main texts where we can learn about Buddhist psychology.

Q: Lama, could you please explain insubstantiality? Is it like dependent arising?

A: Substantiality is actually dependent origination. Insubstantiality is the reversion of dependent origination. So it is like this cup. I can break this cup down into smaller and smaller pieces until we only have the smallest atom. The cup is dependent origination. Because of causes and conditions we have the appearance of this cup. Now if I break this cup into very small pieces, into atoms, then we will lose the cup. So that losing of the cup's identification, or the projection of the cup, is insubstantiality. So in some sense, uncovering that insubstantiality is actually reversing dependent origination.

Q: Lama, in the study of the Abhidharma I have heard there are fifty-one mental factors, and it is the main mind which makes the fifty-second. Is this correct?

A: Yes. Mind, consciousness, and psyche are names that have been used for the same entity, depending upon the times and how we experience them. That's why in Sanskrit the same entity has three different names. The term "chitta" in the word "Bodhichitta" means mind. It is also called "vijnan" which means consciousness. The third name is "manas," which means something similar to "psyche," although it is not a very precise term.

When mind is presently aware of an object, as when we see a visual object through the eyes, then that is called eye consciousness. There are five consciousnesses formed from the five sense organs. Those five are considered sense consciousnesses. But the sixth consciousness, which is the mind consciousness, arises from the basic mind.

Now basic mind is that mind which continues after death and carries on into the next life. Whether there is a physical body or not, mind is continuing all the time. This is the basic mind on which all karma is impressed. All of the emotions are there. Whether we are asleep or arising, there is basic mind. From that basic mind then, with the interdependency between the sense organ and the sense object, these different consciousnesses arise.

Basic mind is immaterial. It is something that lives on by itself after our physical bodies die. It doesn't need to depend upon physical material things. But the consciousness related with the five sense organs will not arise without the physical body.

So these are the different functions of that basic mind. It is continuing from past to present to future, and it is always with those factors. We know the true nature of the mind if we are a great yogi and meditator, and we have seen the clear light.

Once we have seen the true nature of mind, then there are no emotions nor any of those mental factors. Now we have seen the nature of the mind and have gone even beyond the mind. Until then, however, the mind will carry all those emotions.

Mind and mental factors are actually dependent on each other. There are five dependencies we can study. They are dependent on each other, so they are always together. A good example is in the text where it says, "The mind is like the sun and the emotions are like the sunlight."

Q: Lama, is the "basic mind" you talk about the same thing as the "mindstream" I have read about?

A: Yes.

Q: Obviously, you can't have eye consciousness without the mind and without the ego. Once the mind is separated, then the eye consciousness has disappeared?

A: That's right. There are six consciousnesses: eye consciousness, ear consciousness, nose consciousness, tongue consciousness, touch consciousness, and mind consciousness. Mind consciousness continues with the mind even after death because mind consciousness doesn't need a physical organ.

Mind consciousness is present even when we are sleeping and experience clear dreams. Mind consciousness is present even after death when we are in the bardo state. But all five of the other sense consciousnesses depend upon physical organs, and they are dissolved when the physical organs are dissolved at the time of death.

Chapter 2

The Second Noble Truth - The Origin of Suffering

The Second Noble Truth is the origin of suffering. As we have established in the First Noble Truth, the nature of conditioned existence is suffering. The Second Noble Truth looks closely at what the origins of that suffering are.

Origination is more subtle because many times we don't see origination directly. There are lots of misunderstandings and doubts about origination. Buddha also taught four different aspects related to the Second Noble Truth. These aspects help to clear away our misconceptions related to the origin of suffering.

Cause

The first aspect of the Second Noble Truth is cause. This is to help us to see the true source of our pain and suffering. When we experience the suffering of suffering in the form of a headache, we feel the pain of that headache, but we don't know what the real causes are.

We may go to the doctor and receive many different tests. Sometimes a doctor can offer a solution. Other times a doctor may misdiagnose the source of the headache. There can be many different kinds of headaches. There are migraine headaches. There are stress headaches. Some headaches are a warning sign for a stroke. We feel the pain, but the cause can be many different things.

If we look closely, we can see that pretty much all suffering has some cause. But the causes are complex. They are subtle. There are different durations of time we experience these sufferings. Sometimes we cannot remember the causes of our suffering because the suffering has extended over many lifetimes.

There are many reasons why our attempts to determine the causes of suffering can lead to misunderstandings. There are many schools of thought. Perhaps the reason why Buddha taught cause as the first aspect of the Second Noble Truth is because there are many people who don't accept the natural law of karma.

From a medical standpoint, doctors may determine the causes for a physical illness and accept that as the original cause of that particular suffering. Doctors don't necessarily accept karma. So if they find an obvious physical explanation for a particular illness, they may see that as the only cause and rarely look deeper at karmic causes and conditions.

Perhaps the majority of people in the world don't accept karma. That means that people accept only what they can prove, only what they can diagnose materially. But if something is immaterial, then how can they find a diagnosis? The purpose of the first aspect of the Second Noble Truth is to emphasize the natural law of karma.

What is the law of karma? Karma refers to cause, condition, and result. And, within these three, there's interdependency; there is relativity. That is karma. The natural law of cause and effect has the meaning of relativity and interdependency.

Since we don't see the causes and conditions most of the time, many people don't believe in karma. Some people may say "it's karma," but still they may not comprehend the depth of karma. Thus, one reason for this first aspect of "cause" is to prove that everything is interdependent, based on cause, condition, and result.

So all three kinds of sufferings we have outlined in the First Noble Truth are interdependent. They all have causes and conditions. In order to prove this fact, Buddha taught this first aspect of cause.

We can study all the details of different causes, conditions, and results in the Abhidharma, which is actually the most detailed study of the Four Noble Truths. Through extensive study of all of the causes, conditions, and results, we can prove that everything we experience is actually due to karma. As a result of negative karma, we experience suffering.

Everything we experience is due to the interdependency of cause, condition, and result. The first aspect of the Second Noble Truth is to prove that, although everything has a cause, condition, and result, each particular cause will have it's own particular result. If we expect a mango seed to grow into a pomegranate, it will never happen! The result has to have its own cause and condition.

This is how we can prove that all suffering is caused by negative karma based on negative emotions. We can study the various factors of negative karma. We can study the ten negative karmas which correspond to physical, verbal, and mental negative emotions.

Basically we can prove that all suffering is due to negative karma created by negative emotions. This demonstrates that all karma is based on specific causes and conditions. The negative emotions are the seeds; the suffering is the result.

So through this first aspect of cause, we can study karma in general, as well as the causes and results of negative karma. This first aspect, cause, can prove that everything manifests as a result of this cycle of cause, condition and result.

Origination

The second aspect of the Second Noble Truth is "origination." Origination here doesn't mean that karma has an origin or a first cause. Once we've established interdependency and relativity between cause, condition, and result, then within the interdependency we cannot find a first cause. Origination here is actually referring to that cycle where every cause has its own cause, and that cycle keeps repeating again and again.

Each past cause and condition has a present result. Then the present result is the cause and condition for a future result. So this is the cycle through which everything originates. Origination is not to be misunderstood as a "first cause." Origination refutes a first cause. It is referring to interdependent origination, which has a meaning of the result becoming the cause for another chain of events.

In this cycle, one thing can be both the result of something in the past as well as the cause of whatever happens next. So that's why things are interdependently continuing all the time.

So we could say that origination proves that there is no first cause and also no singular cause. Take for example how one entity can be both cause and result. One man can be a son to his own father and also a father to his own son simultaneously. He's one person, but he can be referred to in multiple ways.

In dependent origination, causes are always multiple. They are multiple in the sense that one entity can have different aspects. The entity can be a result, a cause, or a condition, depending on our frame of reference. That's why the second aspect of the Second Noble Truth is to refute the existence of a first cause and also a singular cause.

Everything is unfolding in a cycle, and each thing has multiple aspects. Origination supports the very philosophy of interdependency and the law of karma. So this aspect of origination refers to multiple causes and conditions as well as to interdependency. The main object is to refute a first cause and a singular cause.

Well Produced

The third aspect of the Second Noble Truth has a meaning of "produced" or "well produced." This third aspect is to show that whatever we experience is a direct result of our karma. When we experience suffering, it is because we have participated personally in the creation of that karma.

Whatever suffering we experience is a direct result of our past actions and emotions. Sometimes this extends over multiple lifetimes, so it is difficult for us to see how we have caused it. But it is important to recognize that no one else has produced that karma for us.

When Buddha taught the Four Noble Truths, he was refuting all theistic religions. He asked the question, "If everything was created by God, then why would a benevolent God create so much suffering?" Buddha could not reconcile these opposing factors.

Thus Buddha taught that every suffering we experience, whether it manifests as feelings of pain or of pleasure, must be coming from karma we have personally created.

In order to prove this, Buddha taught this third aspect of the Second Noble Truth. "Well-produced" means that due to our own karma we are now experiencing these sufferings. It has nothing to do with some other force creating such suffering.

This is also related with karmic law. Buddha said that whatever we experience has a direct connection to what we have personally done in the past. All results are due to our own karma and our own emotions.

Another person cannot produce our suffering. We have to have participated in the production of our pain and suffering. To prove that point, Buddha taught this third aspect of the Second Noble Truth. This third aspect, "well-produced," confirms that every experience, every feeling we have, is preceded by our own karma and our own emotions.

Condition

The fourth aspect of the Second Noble Truth is "condition." There are some religious schools like the Jain that believe we have a permanent soul. This permanent soul is said to always be at peace even though circumstantially we have pain and suffering. The Jain believe in a soul which is always happy, and which is free from suffering.

To refute such teachings, Buddha taught about conditions. He observed that all the experiences we have are not only due to our causes but also to our conditions. Causes are like the seed, and conditions are like the water, soil, and everything that makes the seed grow. So you see, causes and conditions are very much related to each other and determine the result.

So this aspect of condition is mainly to refute a permanent cause. In this way Buddha is saying that the Second Noble Truth of origination or causation is a product of causes and conditions. As a result of these causes and conditions we experience suffering.

As we have established, the First Noble Truth is suffering which includes all three kinds of suffering. The Second Noble Truth examines all of the causes and conditions of that suffering.

Generally we see that there are three main causes of suffering: ignorance, desire, and anger. Due to ignorance we create karma. Ignorance is the main cause of birth and rebirth. When we die without any awareness or any practice, when we experience overwhelming pain and suffering at the time of death, we tend to lose consciousness. When the elements of our physical bodies are dissolving at the time of death, we often cannot maintain our awareness. That unconsciousness is, in some sense, an experience of that ignorance. Because we become unconscious at the time of dissolution, we cannot maintain wisdom, we cannot maintain awareness.

Out of that lack of awareness, out of that unconsciousness, when we wake in the bardo intermediate stage after death, those habitual patterns and all that karma that has been impressed on our con-sciousnesses will take over our minds.

All of these afflictive emotions that have been imprinted on our mindstreams will follow us into the bardo. We will carry very strong desire and attachment after death, which will then force our rebirth.

We are conceived and reborn again and again. In that very first moment of conception, when our consciousness is combined with our father's and mother's elements, that is the beginning of the suffering of conditioned nature. The very fact of our birth means we will experience old age and death and will experience the suffering of the conditioned nature of all things.

The Buddhist teachings always discuss death as occurring every

moment. Death is "momentary." From the very moment we are conceived we have started toward death because every moment we are
changing. We can experience that impermanence in every heartbeat.
At any moment that heart can stop, and we can leave this body.

Recently I was talking with a friend who is a doctor. He said that
the more he learned about the workings of human physiology, the
more amazed he was that we live as long as we do! The more he
studied, the more he came to see that our physical bodies are almost
like a ticking time bomb. He was amazed that our bodies function as
well as they do most of the time. At any moment a human body can
stop working.

We have evolved to have this physical body that becomes the
basis for the other two kinds of suffering. If we are never born, then
we don't have a body. However, due to ignorance, we are conceived.
With conception we have physical bodies. Then, with a physical
body, we have the three kinds of suffering. So either way, the
suffering of suffering and the suffering of change are both based on
the suffering of conditioned nature. The basic suffering of conditioned existence is there all the time, even when we don't actively
feel the suffering of change or the suffering of suffering.

Shantideva said, in his Bodhicaryavatara, that most anger is
rooted in pain and suffering. When we have physical pain we may
become short tempered and impatient. Often we express this anger to
the people we are closest to emotionally.

Pain can make adults act like children again. When children have
physical pain, sometimes they act it out on their parents. Maybe
children think they can get away with expressing anger at their
parents since they feel unconditionally loved by them.

It is a common human trait to try to find someone to blame for our suffering. We try to find some kind of excuse by becoming angry at outer circumstances or at someone in our lives.

The other obvious source of suffering occurs when our desires are not being fulfilled. This may also cause us to become angry. And the desire is there in the first place because we do not see the true nature of the object of our desire.

So we can see how the afflictive emotions are completely interdependent. The desire is there because of the ignorance. The unfulfilled desire can cause the suffering. Suffering can be the root of anger. They are all interrelated.

The expression of these three afflictive emotions at a mental level generates karma. At the verbal level, when we express these three emotions, that becomes verbal karma. At the physical level, when we express these three emotions through actions, that becomes physical karma.

We can see how karma and those destructive emotions are the causes and conditions for the three kinds of suffering. The more we understand the way causes and conditions operate, the more we can free ourselves from misconceptions about karma.

On a larger scale, when we accept karma, karma can refute all those big philosophical questions about whether a Creator is responsible for our suffering. When we take personal responsibility for creating our own karma, we can begin to recognize how our karma is creating our experiences of the entire universe. This can encourage us to stop blaming outer circumstances and to begin creating causes and conditions for a positive future.

This is not to diminish how interdependent we are. You see, our personal experiences generated by our individual karmas are also affecting the universe. For this reason it is very important to understand karma - which includes the six causes, five conditions, and four results.

The Buddha taught that one act of killing can have multiple results. One example is that this act of violence may shorten our lives. Furthermore, if we kill with desire, like killing an animal for meat, then that type of killing can increase our desire. If we kill with anger, then that will increase our anger. If we kill with ignorance, that will increase our ignorance.

All these types of killing will also make our habitual pattern of killing stronger. As a result, by killing others, by eliminating their lives, we will experience more lifeless situations in our environments. It will actually affect the energy of our external world. You can really sense this in areas of war or conflict.

Even one act of killing includes all six causes, five conditions, and four different results. Why are there four results? Why are there six kinds of causes?

If we study in depth, then we see that there are many factors involved in even killing one sentient being. For this reason, studying the complexities of karma can be very important. The more we study, the more we can clear away any doubts and misunderstandings. This in turn will give us more and more confidence about the natural law of karma.

So these four aspects of the Second Noble Truth are to clear away all the misunderstandings related with the three sufferings and their causes and conditions.

Q & A

Q: What could be the causes or the origin for a baby to be born with birth defects?

A: Because we live in samsara, we observe that desire, anger, and ignorance are the three main causes of all our suffering.

If we take into account only one lifetime, then maybe it is very hard to prove the causes or the origin for such things one is born with. But as we talked about before, birth and rebirth are a constant cycle. There's no such thing as a first life. Life is beginningless. So that's why there must be many, many multiple causes and conditions related with one's own karma.

Of course these are sometimes related to genetic factors, which are a result of the parent's karmic patterns as well. And even if the parents do not display these defects, their DNA can still carry the karma of their own parents and grandparents. So it can be very difficult to determine a specific cause in such a situation. But what we do know is that all that we experience is a result of our karma. And our karma is determined by these three underlying afflictive emotions of desire, anger, and ignorance here in samsara.

Q: In the case of a baby with birth defects, is it the baby's karma and not the parent's karma? Because you said we are responsible for our own suffering, but other people's karma does cause us suffering too. So we can be the best people, but we are still affected by other's negative karma. So we have to be responsible not only for our own but for other's karma?

A: If others are causing us to suffer, there must be some emotional connection and some karmic participation, even if we cannot recognize it. Without an emotional connection and our own participation, I don't think we will suffer.

Whenever we suffer, and whenever we experience some feeling, it is preceded by our participation in some action or some emotion. That doesn't mean we don't have collective emotions, or we don't do things with others. We do. We have collective karma as a family. We have very strong emotional bonds.

A baby's karma in having those particular parents is, in itself, a strong emotional and karmic connection. There must be something in the past which forced that consciousness to be conceived through those two parents. There must be some very strong attachment or connection.

So because of that, once our emotions are involved, whether it is attachment and love, aversion and anger, or even ignorance, I think they all bring some form of suffering and some form of feeling.

Q: Lama, are you saying that if we get to a certain level, and we don't have these feelings and afflictive emotions, then we won't suffer, regardless of what someone else might do to us?

A: Yes, I think it depends on what kind of feelings you have with someone. Let's say you are very attached to your brother, and you love him very much, then you'll be in lots of pain if he is experiencing pain. But if you hate your brother, maybe you'll be happy if he is experiencing pain!

If you don't have either of these strong feelings, and if you are in a neutral state of ignorance, then you don't have much feeling. So this is how it is with an object. It all depends upon how you react.

These are the three feelings related with an object: love, hate, and indifference. These correspond directly with the three afflictive emotions of attachment, anger, and ignorance.

But we must remember that there are also higher loves. There is compassion. There is equanimity. Sometimes when I have seen lots of pain and suffering and other negative situations, if the family members have some faith and some practice, then adversity can make their faith and practice become even stronger. We can use those difficult situations to cultivate more practice.

Whenever we put ourselves into others' shoes, I think we can feel their pain and suffering. If we imagine someone who's crippled and who cannot walk, we may feel a lot of compassion for them.

Q: Lama I've wondered a lot about the monks and nuns in Tibet that have self-immolated, and the karmic consequences of that. When I think about it, it's a form of killing. It's violence. But on another level, it's on behalf of others that the monks and nuns are drawing attention to the situation. But at the same time, they've taken vows not to kill. So I wonder how to understand this issue?

A: I think it depends on their motivation at the time of death, what kind of emotions they have. If they die with some loving-kindness and compassion, that's good. If they die with so much anger towards China, then it's negative.

If we are highly realized, like the Buddha in a past life, that is one level of transformation. If we read The Jataka Tales, we will know that one time Buddha saw a hungry tigress and her cubs. He felt so much compassion for her that he cut off a bit of his own flesh and gave it to the tigress for her cubs. If we are such a highly realized selfless being, then when we give with all that selflessness, we don't feel much pain. Even when pain is felt, that pain is bearable, and it does not increase our anger and negativities. That relationship to pain increases one's compassion because we see that the pain of others is more acute and we're helping them. So that selfless pain is bearable.

Now if we are not that realized, do we have a purpose? We all have the power to practice patience. If we choose to do so, we all can. But if we don't like something, then even small things can make us feel intense pain. Our approach to pain is relative.

I'm always shocked by those extreme mountain climbers, like the Mt. Everest climbers. Most of these climbers have to be very wealthy in order to make the expedition. Only rich people can climb. It's so expensive to employ many porters and get all the gear. These climbers probably live in very nice mansions. In the winter I doubt they can live without heat in their homes when there's snow outside, and yet they go to Mt. Everest!

Then on Mt. Everest there are so many risks. There are avalanches, storms, and altitude sickness. There are many uncertainties, and often people die. But still people can endure all that hardship when they are determined to climb. So the same people who cannot endure the small cold outside their homes are now willing to give up their lives in pursuit of climbing a mountain.

So what has changed? I think people's mental power and emotional involvements are very strong. In the case of these climbers it is "mind over matter." Positive emotions can be strong, and negative emotions can also be strong.

So these monks and nuns, I hope they die with some kind of positive emotions, but I don't know if it's that way. However, one monk left a message saying, "I'm doing this not just out of desperation. I'm doing this in memory of all the others who have sacrificed their lives before me and also to encourage all the future generations not to lose hope." To increase their courage and their hope, this is why he immolated himself.

Q: Lama, is it only in the desire realm that the mind goes beyond the mind?

A: Yes.

Q: Is that why the higher realms fall down?

A: Yes, that's right. The desire realm is the best realm to practice Dharma. Only desire realm beings can become a Buddha in this life. Beings in the form realm have very good meditation like shamatha meditation, but they don't have good insight meditation. Their shamatha is so good that they sometimes mistake such meditation for nirvāṇa, and they remain in that state of absorption for a long time. But eventually they fall down into the lower realms.

The desire realm is best for practice because the desire realm has six elements. That is the main reason why the desire realm can be transformed. We have the four basic elements as well as the father and mother's white and red elements. So that makes this physical body of the desire realm very suitable for transformation.

The formless realm doesn't have the elements. The form realm doesn't have the parents. In the form realm they don't copulate, so they don't have the white and red elements either. So that's why they don't have the potential to achieve Buddhahood.

Chapter 3
The Third Noble Truth - Cessation

The Third Noble Truth is the truth of cessation. This truth acknowledges that there can be an end to suffering, that we can reach nirvāṇa. While we may try to understand nirvāṇa intellectually, the state of nirvāṇa is actually beyond our intellect. Without a direct experience of nirvāṇa, it is very difficult for us to comprehend what nirvāṇa is. But we will attempt to explore it as scholars and practitioners in order to comprehend the possibility of freedom from suffering.

I often use the example of sugar. Only those of us who have tasted sugar will truly know what sugar is. We cannot reach this experience through discussion or comparison. No matter how many names we use, or how deeply we go into describing its chemical properties, we cannot duplicate the experience intellectually. Even if we were to write a very big book about what sugar is, it still would not give us that firsthand experience.

Nirvāṇa

What is nirvāṇa? Nirvāṇa is the cessation of suffering. That result can only be reached through practicing the Noble Eightfold Path, which will be presented in the Fourth Noble Truth.

As we have discussed, Buddha gave four different aspects to each of the Four Noble Truths. These four aspects are to clear away all our doubts and misconceptions.

Cessation

The first aspect of the Third Noble Truth of nirvāṇa is "cessation" which has a meaning of liberation. This first aspect is to clear away any misunderstandings related to whether freedom from suffering is possible.

If we believe that the destructive emotions, which are the cause of all the sufferings, are inherent in human nature, then no matter how much we practice, we will never be free. If we believe that these afflictive emotions are our true nature, then whatever faith we cultivate, whatever spiritual practice we may do, there will still be no possibility of going beyond suffering and the causes of suffering.

Buddha taught that it is quite the opposite. Buddha said that humans are fundamentally pure by nature. Buddha taught that all sentient beings are possessed of "Buddha nature" and have the potentialities to become free from suffering and the causes of suffering.

Throughout human history there have been two schools of thought. One school thinks that the nature of humanity is passionate and aggressive. This school thinks that humans are wired for war and conflict, imprinted with fight or flight responses, neuroses, and afflictive emotions. There are some who would argue that these responses are embedded in our genes and cannot be altered.

The other school of thought, which is shared by Buddhists, is that by nature we are pure, compassionate, and wise. While Buddhists understand that the nature of life right now is suffering, and suffering has causes, we also perceive that the nature of our minds is free from suffering and free from the causes and conditions of suffering. That inherent nature is actually nirvāṇa.

In the Sutra teachings, that inner space in the mind, that inherent nature, is described as being similar to outer space. When we have lots of clouds and bad weather we don't see the blue sky. And when we have many disturbing emotions and concepts in our minds, then we cannot see the clarity of our inner space either.

Because of these obscurations, we don't experience any nirvāṇa, any cessation. Only on some occasions, when we have a very good deep meditation session, whatever is not real, whatever is relative, whatever is fake, will temporarily dissolve. What remains is the clarity of that inner space.

Outer space is unconditioned. It has been unconditioned for an infinite time in the past. It will be unconditioned for an infinite time in the future. But all the planetary systems, billions of them, come and go. According to the Buddha, these planetary systems are limitless, but none of them are permanent. Only the space is what remains.

Our earth is just one tiny planet, and humans are only one small fraction of the sentient beings on earth. But for us personally, our own experiences are so important that whatever we experience we assume should be a universal truth. We think everyone has to agree with us and has to see reality as we see it. But there is no universal truth to our perceived reality. What we experience is based on our inner conditions. Our individual inner conditions have shaded all of our experiences and have projected a unique experience of the external world.

The universe is limitless. But we interact with the universe based on personal experiences, and those personal experiences are based on our inner conditions. We become very convinced that our individual experience must have some universal authority, but that is not the case.

When we discover that inner space, through meditation, where we transcend all these objects, and where the inner space and the outer space become one, then our experience of everything will change.

When the inner and outer space merge, then for the first time we have a glimpse of nirvāṇa. In addition, we see the absence of all emotions, including the root destructive emotions of anger, ignorance, and attachment.

In this glimpse of nirvāṇa, we see the possibility of complete freedom from suffering. As long as we have feelings, however, we have suffering. Even a happy feeling is suffering according to the Buddha. Even a neutral feeling is suffering.

As we have discussed, when we have pleasure we think we are happy. But that is our misunderstanding of relativity. That is our misunderstanding of karma. Because we experience the result, and we don't see the cause, we think that this is freedom from suffering. But actually karma is such that even those positive feelings can become a cause for negative feelings.

Here in the west when we hear the word "nirvāṇa" we probably think of Kurt Cobain and his famous band "Nirvana" from Seattle. Cobain's life was actually an example of the horrible suffering of samsara. He rose to stardom as a very young man. He sold millions of records around the world. But his fame and wealth only fueled his addictions and increased his suffering.

Artists and musicians are very creative people. They are very sensitive. They work on cultivating an inner space through their art that may even feel like nirvāṇa at times. But the method they are applying is often confused, and the attention they receive often serves to reinforce their destructive emotions. As a result, they can fall down into terrible suffering.

This is what we do in samsara. We try hard to avoid suffering through false methods. In the sixties our culture erupted in a positive revolution fueled by drug use. Some of these psychedelic drugs had the power to give people a glimpse of nirvāṇa. But that high was quickly followed by the withdrawal. There is no shortcut to nirvāṇa. True freedom from suffering can only be reached through deep meditation practice.

Nirvāṇa is a state of not feeling. Pain killers and recreational drugs have the power to temporarily kill feelings in our nervous systems. All systems are shut down, and that's why we may feel some relief, some freedom from suffering. Feeling is based on ego, and when we forget ourselves, we think we are having a wonderful experience. But relief is only temporary when it is achieved in this way. These drugs are not actually freeing us from any of the underlying afflictive emotions.

Our attention always goes to an area that has pain. When we have a headache, all we can think about is that nagging discomfort. If our feelings have been hurt by a friend, all we can think about is that rejection. However, we generally don't carry awareness of or pay attention to areas free from pain.

Many of these drugs are a way to forget ourselves. Because we feel a temporary relief we wonder if it is similar to nirvāṇa. But being momentarily ecstatic or numb, or forgetting ourselves as a result of a drug, has very little in common with the experience of nirvāṇa.

Nirvāṇa is the awareness of a state beyond feeling. The realization of inner space is based on awareness and mindfulness, not distraction. When we go beyond the ego and self, we can become free from all of the five aggregates.

Nirvāṇa is the cessation of the five aggregates. We go beyond the aggregates of form, feeling, ideation, formation, and consciousness. We go beyond our physical bodies. We go beyond our feelings, ideas, and activities.

How can we do that? I think we can only do that through our awareness. We go beyond the ego and self. And then, in the state beyond ego and self, we experience inner space. When we are fully aware of that inner space, we are experiencing nirvāṇa. We are experiencing the cessation of craving and attachment and of all the feelings related with the five aggregates.

"Cessation" means freedom from all the conditioned and unconditioned phenomena. It means freedom from feelings, ideas and activities, including freedom from our minds and emotions. Cessation is possible because that is the nature of our minds when we see that inner space. In that inner space all the aggregates also dissolve.

So the first aspect of the Third Noble Truth, this aspect of cessation, proves that through meditation practice we can experience this freedom. Since we can experience this cessation, then we know there is liberation. We know that there is freedom not only from suffering but from the very causes of suffering.

This aspect of cessation can be very useful in combatting our worldly narcissistic ways of life. It can refute those who don't have any faith in spiritual enlightenment and liberation.

While the Buddha didn't face as much materialism or capitalism as we experience today, there were five prominent non-Buddhist philosophers in India whose misconceptions he was working with.

In particular, there was one non-Buddhist school called "Charvaka" that was very similar to many of our materialistic societies. The Charvakas only believe in this one life. They don't believe in rebirth or karma. Their main purpose in life is to be narcissistic and to pursue pleasure.

The Indian philosopher who founded the Charvaka school had a very clever mind. He developed this whole theory that there is no rebirth, and there's no karma whatsoever. Thus, we can narcissistically enjoy this moment. He thought this pursuit of pleasure was what our lives were comprised of. To refute these philosophers, Buddha taught about this aspect of cessation.

These days Humanism is becoming more popular here at Harvard. Humanists do not have faith in anything which they cannot see or prove. If they don't see rebirth, they cannot believe in it. Everything has to be proven based on direct experience.

Many of us have not seen India yet, but we believe it exists because others have been there. Among the Humanists, there is no belief in any inferential logic. Even today, Buddha's ancient teachings can help to refute these new belief systems, which don't subscribe to karma or rebirth.

Pacification

The second aspect of the Third Noble Truth is called "pacification." We may practice meditation for any number of reasons. Meditation in the Western world is often used for therapeutic purposes. If we practice according to Herbert Benson, we are practicing for the relaxation response. If we practice meditation according to Jon Kabat-Zinn, then the goals of meditation may be mindfulness based stress-reduction. There are many goals for meditation in our current culture.

If we practice shamatha meditation, then maybe we will experience some peace, but this doesn't mean that our peace is permanent. Even the best shamatha practitioners only achieve good awareness and freedom from actively destructive emotions. But shamatha meditation still doesn't free us from sleeping emotions.

Often we misunderstand peace as being equivalent to nirvāṇa. But nirvāṇa is an unconditioned state. It's a permanent state. Even if we experience peace for one whole lifetime, that doesn't mean that we have reached a state of nirvāṇa.

Nirvāṇa is unconditioned, and it is a permanent state once we achieve it. The aspect of pacification makes it clear that these temporary peaceful experiences of meditation, like that state of meditative absorption in the form and formless realms, are not nirvāṇa.

If we are successful in cultivating a good shamatha meditation, that meditation can help us experience a more peaceful mind. But if that shamatha is not integrated with mindfulness meditation, then when we wake up from that shamatha we are still prone to destructive emotions and suffering. This second aspect, pacification, is to clarify that those temporary peaceful states achieved in shamatha meditation are not equivalent to nirvāṇa.

According to Buddhist cosmology, gods such as Brahma, are part of the form realm. Merit accumulated through acts of love, compassion, joy, and equanimity, can help someone to be reborn in the form realm. For this reason they are sometimes called the abode of the Brahma, the "Brahmaviharas."

Someone who has practiced these virtuous qualities without much wisdom, and who has accumulated lots of merit based on such practices, will have a better chance of being reborn in the form and formless realms.

Within Buddhism the form realm is also called the heavenly realm. But that heaven is not a Buddha realm. That heaven has not gone beyond samsara. Those heavenly beings have been reborn there due to lots of merit and positive karma, but still they are missing the wisdom that transcends samsara. They have peace. They have pleasure and happiness. But that peace and happiness is not nirvāṇa. Nirvāṇa is an unconditioned permanent state of cessation.

Immaculate Accomplishment

The third aspect of the Third Noble Truth is "immaculate." This aspect also signifies accomplishment. When we achieve that inner space of nirvāṇa permanently, then that state is immaculate because we have transcended even the causes and conditions of suffering.

This third aspect is also a clarification on formless beings. Yogis who have more merit are reborn in the form realm, the heavenly realm, which we have just discussed. Meditators who are even more accomplished, are reborn in the formless realm. But both the form and the formless beings are still not liberated. They are still not beyond samsara.

In the formless realm, beings do not have physical bodies. They don't have pain or pleasure, happiness or unhappiness. They only have neutral mental feelings and very subtle concepts in the mind.

For this reason, meditation is much deeper in the formless realm. It is a state of absorption, free from all active and gross feelings and thoughts. But the mind maintains a level of attention. This state of absorption is also called "samadhi."

This third aspect of the Third Noble Truth is to clarify that such states of absorption are not nirvāṇa. Even if formless beings were to remain in samadhi for eons, when they emerged from meditation, suffering could still arise, and they could still experience disturbing emotions. This experience of absorption is not an unconditioned state. Only nirvāṇa is immaculate, pure, and unconditioned.

Going Beyond or Renouncing Samsara

The fourth aspect of the Third Noble Truth is "going beyond" or "renouncing" samsara. Samsara is the endless cycle of life and death that we experience. This cycle of suffering is depicted by the Buddhist image of the Wheel of Life. Samsara is not limited to our small planet earth. Due to our karma and emotions, we are reborn again and again in the desire, form and formless realms, throughout countless planetary systems.

Nirvāṇa is when we go beyond the samsara of these three realms. It is full renunciation. As long as we experience feelings of any kind, even of profound peace, we are still not in a state of nirvāṇa. Only when our spiritual practice and meditation have the power to go beyond samsara's three realms, will we experience the complete cessation of suffering.

As long as we have an ego, we cannot go beyond the three

realms. Ego causes the emotions of ignorance, attachment, and anger to arise. Out of these root destructive emotions, we create so much karma.

Due to interdependency we are cycling again and again through countless lifetimes. Only when we see the true nature of ego, only when we are egoless, will we be free from destructive emotions. But as long as we are attached to ourselves, we won't have renunciation. Only when we reverse the Wheel of Life, only when we overcome ignorance through deep meditation, can we achieve nirvāṇa.

Buddha taught these four aspects of the Third Noble Truth in order to clear away all the misunderstandings and doubts about nirvāṇa. Nirvāṇa is reached through the Noble Eightfold Path presented in the Fourth Noble Truth.

Q &A

Q: Lama, if a person accumulates a vast amount of merit but hasn't achieved full shamatha meditation, could that person only be born in the desire realm? And if that person accomplishes perfect shamatha meditation, can that person be reborn now in the form realm?

A: Yes.

Q: So if a person accomplishes the four concentrations of shamatha meditation in the form realm, is that a requisite for the formless realm? How can a person be reborn in the formless realm?

A: One will be reborn in the formless realm only when shamatha becomes deeper and deeper through meditative absorption. The four levels of the formless realm are as follows: first, there is the absorption of limitless space; second is absorption of limitless consciousness; third is absorption of nothingness; fourth is absorption of non-ideation.

As long as meditation is in the form and formless realms, there is still no insight meditation. That is why these yogis are still in samsara. So these levels of shamatha meditation in reference to an object become more and more refined at each level. That can make the difference and can define these different stages.

Q: Lama, do the three schools go through the nirvāṇa stage, or is it just the Hinayana?

A: Just the Hinayana.

Q: So the Vajrayana would jump from where to where?

A: That's a very good question, very helpful. Between the Mahayana and the Vajrayana, philosophically, there is no difference. Actually, Vajrayana is part of the Mahayana system. The only difference is in the method of practice. Within the Hinayana, the result is to go beyond samsara, to achieve nirvāṇa. Mahayana and Vajrayana not only go beyond samsara, but also go beyond nirvāṇa. So we have to go beyond two times. That's why the result of Mahayana and Vajrayana is called complete Buddhahood. Because the result is to go beyond samsara, as well as nirvāṇa.

Q: But how can you go beyond nirvāṇa if you've never been in it? And would it be a bad thing to be in it?

A: If we go through nirvāṇa, then to go beyond nirvāṇa usually takes a longer time. It will take a much longer time because it is almost as if those who go beyond samsara through nirvāṇa take a wrong exit. So it takes much longer!

Whether we will go to nirvāṇa or not is based on our practice. If we have, from the beginning, taken the Bodhisattva vow, that will determine whether our result will be to go to nirvāṇa or to full enlightenment.

Those who have taken the Bodhisattva vow, due to the power of compassion and bodhicitta, will be helped by this vow and these powers to go beyond nirvāṇa. See, nirvāṇa is only wisdom. So that's why it's a permanent state from which we don't come back. We don't reincarnate because we didn't create the resolution to have compassion arise through our practice. That's why it's a permanent state, in which a person remains all the time. In full enlightenment a person has wisdom, and out of such wisdom a person has limitless compassion. Out of that compassion, such a person also reincarnates to help other sentient beings.

So that's the difference. Within the Hinayana tradition, from the very beginning, it's all negative. The disciplines are framed in terms of renunciations: not killing, not stealing, non-harming, all based on negative terminology. There is no compassionate bodhicitta aspect. So that's why it's a permanent state from which there is no reincarnation.

Q: So it has to be permanent?

A: Yes. It will be determined by whether or not we have generated the resolution for self-liberation and taken the Bodhisattva vow.

Q: Can a person who has taken the Bodhisattva vow be transformed through vipassana meditation?

A: You have taken the Bodhisattva vow?

Q: Yes.

A: And then you practiced vipassana?

Q: Yes, but not very strongly. My Vipassana practice is not well developed.

A: Whether a practice will become Hinayana or Mahayana is all dependent upon our resolution. If we take the Bodhisattva vow, then our vipassana and shamatha meditations become Mahayana practices. If we only take the Pratimoksha vow, then such practices become Hinayana. As many people do these days, if we practice vipassana insight meditation or shamatha, without any resolution, then it will become a worldly meditation and not a spiritual one.

That is what I mean, for example, regarding stress reduction and all these other forms of meditation. They are meditations, but they are not spiritual because they will not help us go beyond samsara. Such meditations will only help us reduce stress, relax, or have peace in samsara. That's why these forms of meditation are called worldly. It's the same meditation, but the results we achieve are dependent upon our motivation and our resolution, and upon how they are generated. That will make the difference. So the same meditation can be worldly, can be Hinayana, or can be Mahayana depending on our resolution.

Chapter Four
The Fourth Noble Truth - The Path

The Fourth Noble Truth is the Noble Eightfold Path. This path leads to self awakening and ultimately to the cessation of suffering. It offers us eight principle guidelines to live by. These eight include: right view, right intention, right speech, right action, right livelihood, right effort, right mindfulness, and right concentration.

"Path" in this context has a meaning of realization based on our practice. Generally in Buddhism, we refer to five different levels of the path, starting with the path of accumulation that begins when we take refuge. We accumulate merit by doing our practices again and again, whether they are related with meditation or with keeping precepts or are based on wisdom trainings.

Part of the path of accumulation is accumulating merit by doing daily practices. By practicing repeatedly, we counteract negative karma and the actions which cause destructive emotions. Through the path we come to the result that is the state of nirvāṇa we have just discussed. So the path starts with the path of accumulation. Second is the path of application. As our practice becomes stronger and stronger, we can overcome negative actions and destructive emotions more easily.

Within our minds, there is always a conflict between positive and negative emotions and actions. Before we develop a spiritual practice, our destructive emotions and negative karma are often strongest. These negative emotions and actions form habitual patterns and also determine our personalities. But once we commit to the spiritual path, our positive karma and positive emotions grow stronger and stronger through our practice.

The path of application has four different levels. These four levels are: heat, summit, patience, and excellent Dharma. These levels are the measurement of how much merit we have accumulated and how much negative karma we have burned and purified.

When our accumulation of merit becomes very strong, and we burn off all our negative karma, we may see a glimpse of self-lessness, a glimpse of emptiness. That glimpse is our entry into the path of seeing. The Noble Eightfold Path, which is the essential feature of the Fourth Noble Truth, is part of the realization of the path of seeing.

When a yogi has a glimpse of emptiness, of selflessness, then for the first time wisdom can arise. That realization can happen only when we have purified our negative karma and overcome our active destructive emotions. Only then may we have a glimpse of empti-ness.

The Path of Seeing: A Glimpse of Emptiness

The first aspect of the Fourth Noble Truth is the path of seeing the emptiness or selflessness. Based on this insight, we continue to see that emptiness or selflessness more and more in our meditation.

This glimpse of emptiness gives us profound understanding and faith in the path. It invigorates our practice since we become absolutely convinced that we can achieve the result, the nirvāṇa. It also helps us to overcome any misconceptions and any false belief in a permanent self.

When Buddhist yogis glimpse the truth of selflessness, they become utterly confident that there is no such thing as a permanent self. The nature of the self is selflessness. This is very critical, critical not only philosophically, but also critical in proving that there is nirvāṇa, which is the cessation of the self.

This cessation of the self includes the cessation of all five aggregates as well. Even the fifth aggregate, which is the mind and mental consciousness, is also ceased.

When all these defiled aggregates are ceased, then a yogi will not perceive any permanent self. What is realized instead is the wisdom of selflessness. Only the wisdom remains.

This is why the Noble Eightfold Path is important. As we have discussed, there are five levels to the path. There are the two worldly levels of accumulation and application, and then there are three noble levels.

When we speak of these levels in the context of the Fourth Noble Truth, we are generally referring to those three noble levels: the path of seeing, the path of meditation, and the path of no more learning.

The first worldly level, accumulation, is about recognizing the path. This brings us confidence that there is a way forward which can help us realize nirvāṇa. We realize that through the second worldly level of application we can apply the dharma practice and gain insight. This paves the way for the three noble levels of the path: the path of seeing, the path of meditation, and the path of no more learning.

The spiritual path is not a linear trajectory. Rather, it is a progression through different states of mind. The path is a method to evaluate and guide our realizations.

Appropriate or Suitable

The second aspect of the Fourth Noble Truth is "appropriate" or "suitable." Whenever we have a certain realization in the mind, this aspect helps us to see what is possible and what is not possible. For example, when we glimpse our own selflessness, then we see that selflessness is possible, and that self-clinging is not appropriate.

If we look within the mind, there are things to be abandoned, and there are things to be realized. But that is all still within the mind. When we go beyond the mind, there is nothing to realize. Even if we study Buddhist psychology according to the two levels of the Abhidharma, the study still cannot encompass all the complexities of the mind.

The mind is very intricate and filled with contradictory thoughts and emotions. Love is in the mind. Hate is also in the mind. Both are existing, but the two are completely opposite. The same is true with jealousy. Jealousy is there, and joy is also there. All the conflicting emotions are there. There are destructive feelings, positive feelings, and neutral feelings.

As we follow the Buddhist path, we start to understand that spiritual practice helps us to abandon many negative activities and mental states. Through this process of abandonment and renunciation, we start to make space for great realizations to occur.

If we study all the mental activities according to the ancient Buddhist texts of the Abhidharma, we will learn that there are ten basic natural activities of the mind that are always present. There are also negative emotions like ignorance and attachment, and positive emotions of love and compassion.

Buddhist practice relies on cultivating positive emotions.

Through focusing on positive emotions, we learn to gradually over-come the negative ones. We are working towards uncovering the natural qualities of the mind which are wisdom and compassion.

So this aspect of "suitability" means that all the emotions and mental activities are not permanent. They are there to be trans-formed. Through the practice we abandon that which is to be abandoned, and then we begin to see the inherent qualities of the mind.

The mind is very complex. We need the mind in order to accomplish our spiritual journey. But ultimately, through practice, we can achieve nirvāṇa, that state in which the mind ceases to exist.

You may wonder what is left after the mind ceases. What is left is wisdom. When we go beyond the mind, then only wisdom remains. This second aspect of "suitability" or "appropriateness," informs our practice. As we progress along the spiritual path, we can use this aspect to determine what must be abandoned, and what can be achieved.

Achieving or Attaining

The third aspect of the path is "achieving" or "attaining." When we talk about achievement in this context, we don't mean achieve-ment on a mental level. What we are really talking about is achievement based on wisdom, based on recognizing the true nature of the mind itself. As we abandon more and more negative activities and emotional states, we begin to achieve this inherent wisdom.

The second aspect we just discussed of "suitability" has more to do with method, with the means of accomplishing. But this third aspect, that of attainment, is about achieving nirvāṇa. We are practicing in order to achieve freedom from suffering.

When we go beyond the mind, we call this "achievement" or "attainment." But this accomplishment is very different from the way we think of achievement in our ordinary lives. Through abandoning all our negative karma and destructive emotions we can discover the very nature of our minds. Uncovering that wisdom is the extraordinary "achievement" this third aspect is describing.

The Four Noble Truths are primarily taught in the Hinayana tradition of Buddhism. According to this tradition, nirvāṇa is the ultimate accomplishment. However, the Four Noble Truths have also been adopted by the Mahayana and the Vajrayana traditions of Buddhism, in which the ultimate goal is quite different.

The Mahayana tradition puts great emphasis on the Bodhisattva path, in which we aim to free not only ourselves but all beings from suffering. We take the Bodhisattva vow that we will continue to take rebirth in order to help others. The ultimate achievement in both Mahayana and Vajrayana is full enlightenment.

Full enlightenment is not the same as nirvāṇa. Nirvāṇa is the accomplishment of wisdom alone. But full enlightenment includes compassion. According to the Mahayana and Vajrayana traditions, enlightenment is the union of both wisdom and compassion.

The results of our practice will be determined by whatever vows we have taken. The Hinayana vow of Pratimoksha emphasizes self-liberation as the ultimate state. If we take that vow we can achieve liberation in nirvāṇa.

In the Mahayana tradition, we take the Bodhisattva vow. We promise to practice for the sake of all sentient beings. Due to this vow we can achieve full enlightenment, the union of wisdom and compassion. But when we achieve full enlightenment, we effortlessly reincarnate in order to continue to help other beings.

Vajrayana practitioners take the Samaya vow. But the Samaya vow cannot be taken without the Pratimoksha and the Bodhisattva vows. Vajrayana encompasses all three vows. When we achieve the stage of a yidam, a fully enlightened being, then we have the same power to effortlessly manifest to help other sentient beings.

The only difference between the Mahayana and Vajrayana is the path. Vajrayana offers us more elaborate and varied practice methods than Mahayana does. The resulting enlightenment, however, is basically the same. So this third aspect of the path, the aspect of "achievement," will differ based on the Buddhist path we practice and the vows we take.

Liberation or Deliverance

The fourth aspect of the path is "liberation" or "permanent "deliverance." Through our diligence and practice, the path has the power to deliver us to complete freedom from suffering and the causes of suffering.

The term "deliverance" in this context also means cessation. In this final stage, we go beyond all karma and emotions. The path has the power to free practitioners completely from suffering and the causes of suffering.

Q & A

Q: Lama, it doesn't seem very simple to reverse ... If we just get rid of our feelings through our meditation and go beyond them, then that is what starts the reversal?

A: I think at this point it will be very hard for us to just drop our feelings. Feelings are part and parcel of our lives and are part of our physical bodies as well as our minds. On the spiritual path the most critical thing is to notice that we have this aspirational part of who we are. We all are longing for happiness. We all are longing for pleasure. While that is the goal, the issue is how we pursue pleasure and how we pursue happiness.

With what emotions are we chasing these objects or feelings of pleasure? If we take a moment to reflect, we realize that while attaining pleasure and happiness may bring some temporary enjoyment, this pursuit is also sowing seeds of future pain and suffering because nothing is permanent.

So when we study the First Noble Truth of suffering, we see how feelings bring more problems. The First Noble Truth of suffering is basically a study of feelings. Buddha is saying that even pleasure is suffering. Even happiness is suffering. So that is big. What we are pursuing in our worldly lives, and what the Buddha with his meditation and profound insight discovered, are two very different things.

Buddha saw the truth. If we can have some confidence in that truth, then we will come to understand that even pleasure is suffering; even happiness is suffering. And then, although we have feelings, such feelings will not make us be caught in a karmic chain reaction.

Instead, that knowing itself, has the power to free us from karma. This is most critical. Renunciation is a result of our understanding of the truth of suffering in samsara.

Once we understand completely about the suffering that even positive feelings generate, then at some point we will no longer be pursuing feelings so obsessively and with such attachment. This is how we begin to erase some of our ignorance. For the first time we will experience some freedom.

This recognition of the suffering related to our feelings is the beginning of the spiritual path. So that's why all paths say that without renunciation, there is no spiritual path. Renunciation is based on recognizing all the suffering in samsara. That suffering includes pleasure, happiness, and even neutral feelings. We must renounce all feelings.

As long as we have destructive emotions and negative karma, we will produce these feelings. Feelings are not reliable, but still we pursue them. As a result we are caught in cyclic existence.

Q: If a person receives a transmission of phowa at the time of death, will that person be achieving a state of deliverance because he or she does not dwell anymore in cyclic existence?

A: That depends on the effectiveness of the phowa. If the phowa is very effective, and the consciousness is delivered to a pure realm, then maybe there is a deliverance. That is the goal of doing phowa. Phowa is to transfer consciousness into a pure realm. So if the phowa is completely effective in that way, it's possible.

Q: Lama, why is it so wonderful for a Bodhisattva to feed himself to a hungry tiger as we learn about in that Buddhist story? It seems to me that once he has fed himself to a creature of desire, then he can't help other sentient beings.

A: That is a story based on a past incarnation of Buddha as a Bodhisattva, so there must be some karmic link. A Bodhisattva who is giving parts of his or her body to a hungry tigress, is helping another suffering being wholeheartedly, without any ego, without any self-clinging. Bodhisattvas are just there to help. Suddenly, if that Bodhisattva has some realization of emptiness, then there is the perfection of giving. In that emptiness there is no giver, no gift, and no receiver. Then, whether a Bodhisattva is helping one tiger or helping all sentient beings, it is the same. There is no receiver. There is no giver. And there is no gift in that state of emptiness, in that perfection of giving.

Now at our relative level, with our egos, it would be very difficult to give our flesh to a tiger. Our egos are involved even when we give a little bit of blood. It can be so painful. But for a Bodhisattva who has achieved emptiness, those questions, I think, are irrelevant.

Q: I am working hard in my life now so that, if I am lucky enough, maybe later in life I can do nothing but practice, retreat, or become a monk, or study alone. When I'm working in this worldly world now, and I have so much to take care of, and so much to do, and

even just taking care of myself takes away from my Dharma study-
ing, sometimes this causes me some frustration. I know I should not
be frustrated, but what kind of attitude should I have? How can I
turn this frustration and this desire to be able to study the Dharma
into something positive? How can I take that frustration and desire
and use it?

A: It seems like your frustration is because you want to practice, and
there is no conducive condition to do that, so you have frustration.
We have to do what we can. We cannot do something that is beyond
us. At this point we have to take care of our lives. We need to eat
food. We need to read books. We need shelter and all those things.
Without those things it's hard to live. Without living, we cannot
practice.

There are different approaches. In Tibetan Buddhism, in
Mahayana Buddhism, it's not necessary to live an isolated life to
practice. See, it all depends on our motivation.

Sometimes our motivation is good, and even if we are living
daily life in the world, we can have serious spiritual practices. When
there are more challenges, those challenges can be used as part of
our spiritual practices. If one can go away for a whole lifetime, that's
one thing. But even if we go on retreat for years, when we come
back we still have to deal with the world. And if we cannot deal, that
can also be difficult. So spiritual retreat does not guarantee us
progress.

All this frustration can be helpful to our practice. Wherever we
are, in whatever situation, we can use that situation for whatever
practice we can cultivate. That is something for us to consider. Then,

when we have the opportunity, we can go on retreat. We have to use whatever our situation is to further our practice. It is hard to achieve an ideal situation if we just wait for an ideal situation to present itself to us.

The most important thing is our motivation. We should try to do a daily practice in whatever time we have. If we have a sadhana practice or some daily meditation, this will really help us to overcome and break our habitual patterns. Then, when the situation is improved, we can expand on these practices.

We cannot be dreamers. Some of my students have completed long retreats. Some of my students have even done three year retreats. Then in the end, when they came back to the world, they could not fit into the world anymore. They could not earn a living, and they became more frustrated! They could not get a job. They could not support themselves. At some point they went into retreat to produce renunciation from the world, but now they came back from the retreat saying, "I wish I hadn't gone!"

We have to be practical. If we are practicing Mahayana and Tantra, then whatever our situation is in life, we try to use it. That can challenge us, and in some sense, those challenges can be difficult. But those challenges can also be very helpful. If there is no challenge, it is too easy.

You may have heard the story of that one yogi trying to practice patience. Then somebody challenged him by slapping him. This was a very good test of the level of his practice!

So until then, you never know. Do your daily practice. If you have Ngondro practice, you should finish your Ngondro practice. Do one hundred thousand refuge, one hundred thousand prostrations, one hundred thousand Vajrasattva mantra, one hundred thousand Mandala Offerings. You don't need to go into long retreats to do those practices. You can do those over weekends, or even as a daily commitment. Do those foundation practices, the Ngondro practices, for many years. They are practical.

Chapter Five
The Noble Eightfold Path - Right View

We have already discussed the four aspects of the Fourth Noble Truth. Now we will examine the path more closely. The Fourth Noble Truth is the Noble Eightfold Path leading us from suffering. This path has eight factors which can guide us on the way.

Right View

The first branch is Right View, which is the most important part of the Noble Eightfold Path. It is the most important because Right View is related to wisdom which overcomes ignorance. In order to realize Right View, however, we have to investigate the wrong view.

Buddha taught that there are five wrong views. Wrong views are those misconceptions through which our defilements are increased. The first wrong view is seeing the five aggregates as the basis of the self. The first wrong view has a meaning of projecting ego onto the five aggregates. We project some inherent permanence of the self and ego onto these five aggregates of form, feeling, ideation, formation, and consciousness.

First Right View: Selflessness of Self and Phenomena

To counter the first wrong view of "satkayadrsti," Buddha offered the first right view of the selflessness of oneself and phenomena.

We all cling very strongly to the self and ego. The Madhyamika masters emphasized that the source of suffering in samsara is this attachment. They observed that first we cling to the self; then we cling to all the objects we possess, whatever we call "mine" in our universe. With these two wrong views of "self" and "mine," we produce very strong clinging, and all our destructive emotions are increased.

Those who are on the path of seeing and have seen the aspect of emptiness for the first time will see that this clinging to the self and to the five aggregates is only relative. It is not an ultimate truth. We are born with an ego, and we spend much of our lives reinforcing that ego. But those yogis who are on the path of seeing realize that the ego is just a relative projection.

As we look deeper and deeper on the path of seeing, we begin to have a glimpse of emptiness for the first time. In this glimpse we realize that what we have projected is only relative; it is not inherently existing. Ultimately we cannot find any permanent self. That's why all these projections are part of a wrong view. We begin to realize that ultimately we cannot find any inherent existence in the five aggregates.

If we look for a permanent self in each of the five aggregates, we cannot find any proof. When we study the great teachings of The Heart Sutra, we see the nature of the five aggregates. The Sutra says, "Form is emptiness, emptiness is form; form is no other than emptiness, emptiness is no other than form." In this way the Sutra breaks down all our assumptions about the five aggregates.

When we look closely at the first aggregate of "form," from the gross level of the human body, right down to the cellular or atomic level, we cannot find the self.

When we look into the second aggregate, that of "feeling," we also cannot find a self. When we examine the third aggregate of "ideations," we also cannot see any inherently existing self in all our thoughts.

If we continue on to the fourth aggregate of "formations," we learn that there are over fifty different kinds of mental activities included in this aggregate. Even if we look into every single one of them, we cannot find any evidence of a self. Even if we look into the mind, into that fifth aggregate of "consciousness," we cannot find the self or ego.

Now, due to our strong emotions, we become incredibly attached to our sense of self. If we look closely at our lives, we begin to see how much energy we invest in building up and protecting this ego. We are projecting a self, interdependently, based on the five aggregates.

Only through meditation, when we see the emptiness in all five aggregates, will we also see the true emptiness nature of the self. So whenever we project a sense of self, it is actually a wrong view. Wrong view is having emotional involvement with a sense of self in reference to the five aggregates. So Buddhists would consider the Hindu belief in a permanent self or "atman" to be a wrong view.

Now on the other hand, when we see selflessness for the first time, then we understand right view. In order to know what right view is, we need to fully recognize our wrong view. Wrong view includes not only belief in the personal self but also all of our self-references. This includes all of the objects which we consider "mine." We can only own something if we believe we exist in the first place!

This involvement with our possessions is also based on the five aggregates. This applies to all of our attachments, material and mental, related to this idea of "mine." We say, "my car" or "my child" or "my country," and we believe that all of these are existing in relation to ourselves. Until we see the emptiness in all the phenomenal objects, as well as in ourselves, we will still be trapped in our wrong views.

For this reason Buddha taught the selflessness of the person and the selflessness of phenomena. Yogis and meditators on the path of seeing recognize the inherent selflessness and emptiness of all things. This is the first right view.

Second Right View: Belief in Karma

To counter the second wrong view of "mithyadrsti" we must first examine our misunderstandings related with karma. We may talk about karma all the time, but there are many misconceptions. We don't see the truth of cause and result. We often overlook the inter-dependency between cause and result on the relative level.

Of course ultimately things are beyond interdependency. There are two levels to everything, the relative level and the ultimate level. Every object has relative interdependency and ultimate emptiness nature.

Take a bell for example. A bell has relative interdependency. There are causes and conditions that produced the bell. But the true nature of the bell is emptiness. There are two aspects to each object. What we will see is dependent on how we are looking into that object and on the level of our meditation experience.

If we don't believe in interdependency on the relative level, then we don't believe in karma. Not believing in karma cuts all the roots of our virtues and merits. If we don't believe in cause and effect, then we have no motivation to increase our positive activities. It is vital to our spiritual practice that we recognize the truth of interdependency in the relative world.

Without belief in karma, there is a risk that we will become nihilists. In the Buddha's time, in India, there were some non-Buddhist schools that did not believe in karma. As a result they also did not believe in rebirth. Buddha taught about karma in order to counter these misconceptions.

Failure to believe in karma is the second wrong view. We live in the relative world. We live in interdependency. We must go through the interdependency in order to see emptiness. If we don't believe in interdependency, then it is unlikely we will realize emptiness. It is also unlikely that we will cultivate all the positive spiritual qualities and good merit necessary to gain realization.

Belief in interdependency and karma has to do with natural law. If we don't believe in natural law, then there is disharmony on a fundamental level. If we don't believe in karma, we will also not believe in rebirth. If we believe that we are only living for this one lifetime, then we will have very little incentive to accumulate merit or to do virtuous deeds that don't immediately benefit us.

As I have mentioned, the very reason the Charvaka philosophy was developed was to permit people to indulge their appetites and to become more narcissistic. According to that philosophy then, even killing or stealing is permissible in the pursuit of pleasure. There is no belief in karma; therefore, the Charvakas have no concern about the consequences of their actions. They believe only in momentary feelings, and in whatever actions will bring them pleasure. The Charvakas are known to be the most narcissistic philosophers. Buddha taught this second right view in order to help lift their ignorance regarding karma.

Third Right View: Freedom from Extreme Views

To counter the third wrong view of "antagrahadrsti" we can use our understanding of the interdependency of the relative world to see the ultimate truth of emptiness. It is a right view if we also use emptiness to understand that we live in interdependency in a relative world. Only through truly understanding relativity will we see emptiness.

This is the reason why we have to do all this accumulation of merit and the preliminary Ngondro practices. The Ngondro practices are based on karma. We accumulate good karma in order to purify negative karma. The ultimate aim is to go beyond karma altogether to see emptiness.

The third wrong view is when we have extreme views about our own conclusions. If we have concluded, through study and analysis, that our philosophical stance is superior, then we become attached to that conclusion. It is a wrong view to believe that our ideas are the best.

This is the fundamental problem at the root of religious extremism and fanaticism. Terrible atrocities have been committed throughout history based on the belief that "My God is better than your God." Many wars have been fought in order to defend a belief that "my view is the best."

We can find these extremes in religion and within various

philosophical schools. Within Buddhism, we have four philosophies: Vaibhasika, Sautrantika, Mind Only, and Madhyamika. Each one of these philosophical stances can lead a philosopher to an extremist position. This is a danger within all the Tibetan traditions. There are many debates among philosophers. These philosophers have all determined that their own conclusions are the best.

This is also a great danger for Buddhist scholars. This intellectual attachment to particular views can often be a huge impediment to meditation practice. This kind of extremism may help to spread knowledge and scholarship, but it can be counterproductive to spiritual practice. The purpose of Buddhist scholarship is threefold: first to study, next to reflect, and then to practice. Practice must free us from extremism and liberate us from all of this clinging.

Now, if we are clinging to the very method that we are using to liberate ourselves, then that is one of the worst attachments. It can prevent us from any true realization.

Sometimes the best scholars have the biggest egos. This is true in religion and in academia. If scholars have not used that knowledge to transform themselves, if they have not seen the wisdom within all the ideas they have collected, then there is very little growth and realization. They become trapped by their own intellects.

This is why we have so much fighting over the "isms." We see this conflict between all the religions as well as between communism and capitalism. All these "isms" have something to do with coming to a particular conclusion.

If we become very attached to a particular conclusion, then there is the potential to become extreme. We can become extreme in our views based on either eternalism or nihilism.

Within theistic religion, eternalism can be a great danger. This is where we see the view that, "My God is the supreme God. My God is the best." We bring God into the realm of our own egos, projecting a sense of ownership over God.

As a result we find any opposing view to be a direct threat. This is how we decide that "My God is the only God. Your God is the bad one." We are fighting over God. Would God really want it that way? We lower God to our level, and basically this becomes a fight of the ego!

Buddha warns us against any extreme view. Of course even atheism can become an extreme. Recently I saw a news story about Humanists in New York who bought a billboard in a Jewish Orthodox neighborhood and wrote in Hebrew saying something to the effect that "Your God is just a myth." These same Humanists also bought a billboard in New Jersey and wrote a similar message in Arabic, insulting the Muslims. So we see that even the Humanists can fall into an extreme.

If we are attached to "our" God, we don't even realize that we don't know who God really is until we are very enlightened. Until then our egos are making God something very permanent. As a result we are waging war and fighting constantly.

So eternalism can be a wrong view. Nihilism is also a wrong view. This absence of belief in anything is equally extreme. Within any of the Buddhist philosophies, if someone thinks his or her view is the only "right one," then in reality it is a wrong view. Tibetans think they have the highest and best Buddhist philosophy of Madhyamika. Within the highest Madhyamika, then the Tibetan scholars debate which conclusion is the best between "self-emptiness," "other emptiness," and "emptiness free from the four extremes." This argument has lasted for many centuries, and it still continues today.

Scholars cling to their own views. Those who believe in "other emptiness" think they are the best. Those who explain emptiness according to "freedom from the four extremes" think they are the best. There are three groups even among the Tibetan schools. It's an ongoing argument. But the great yogis, the great meditators, are focused on their practice and really don't worry about these arguments.

This third wrong view is extremism, the wrong view of being an extremist who clings to a particular conclusion of an opinion or idea. Yogis who are gaining realization on the path of seeing realize that ultimate reality is free from all the extremes.

Buddha reiterated again and again that wisdom is inexpressible. Wisdom is beyond words, beyond expression. Most of the time we will fall into one of the extremes the moment we try to express wisdom through words. If we read all the Sutras, we even find contradictions in Buddha's teachings. This is a result of Buddha teaching to a particular audience at a particular time. He would teach in a way that was most appropriate to those in attendance.

That's why there were said to be three turnings of the wheel. This was a graduated path, designed to lead people slowly towards some understanding. Buddha knew that if he explained emptiness to people who had no other Buddhist foundation, that the truth of emptiness could be very shocking and terrifying. Buddha realized that people might even become too frightened to practice.

That's why Buddha's teachings lead step by step. But when

describing ultimate reality, Buddha said it's free from all the extremes. We cannot express this ultimate reality, but it is something we can realize through great practice.

For those who have realized ultimate reality, that wisdom cannot be expressed. Understanding freedom from the four extremes is the best reference we can have for that experience. But the reference cannot give us the experience. Only meditation can offer us this realization of wisdom. Clinging to any of the four extremes of existence, non-existence, both or neither, is the third wrong view.

Fourth Right View:
Not Esteeming Our Own Spiritual Practices and Disciplines as the Supreme

To counter the fourth wrong view of "shilavrataparamarsha" we should be careful not to cling to, nor esteem, any of our practices as being supreme. Whether we have taken Pratimoksha vows, or Bodhisattva vows, or Samaya vows, we must be very careful not to think that our disciplines are the best.

Practice and discipline should be methods to go beyond the emotions. But if we get too attached to our methods, then they will not liberate us. There are many cautionary stories about such attachments.

This is something for those Buddhists who are doing a daily sadhana practice to really contemplate in their meditation. Why do we do the generation stage practice? After reciting the mantra, why do we then have to do the completion stage practice and meditation beyond thought? Why can't we just stay in that deity's form?

See, we have to go beyond that subtle attachment to the divine and to the form of the deity we are practicing. That's why we must do the completion practice. If we get too attached to the method and to the deity, then that method can actually increase our egos. Instead of helping us to become free and liberated, our practice can bind us. That's how it can become a wrong view. We will never realize the path of seeing if we are too attached to our practices.

Fifth Right View:
Not Esteeming Our Own Conclusions or Views as the Supreme

To counter the fifth wrong view of "drstiparamarsha," one should not think or esteem one's own conclusions or views as being the best. One Tibetan scholar said something interesting. He said, "In the end, we become extremists because we draw philosophical conclusions based on our extreme attachments which are rooted in the ego." This implies that no matter how much we study and practice, until we are enlightened we will only have limited understanding, and thus we will still fall into an extreme.

Knowledge is based on ego. That's why knowledge is not wisdom. We bring our understanding to these studies at the level of our egos, and then we get attached to those views. Then we use the philosophies of Tibetan and Indian Masters and of the Buddha himself to substantiate our views, but none of this is based on our own realization and liberation.

When scholars do academic research they sometimes talk about uncovering "original" truths related to Buddha's teachings. But how original are these truths? In the context of their research studies it is based on ego more than on enlightened wisdom.

Intellectual study is based on relative information and knowledge. We present some new findings, and then we believe that what we have done is authentic and original. But none of these academic findings are based on insight wisdom. They are based more on research in the material relative world, and on synthesizing information from various places. So our own extreme attachment to a conclusion can be a wrong view.

We have to recognize the five wrong views in order to correct them. Through our meditation practices we move beyond the paths of accumulation and application to reach that third path, the path of seeing. It is on this third path that we see these views are wrong, and for the first time we will have a glimpse of Right View. This is called "noble view" because for the first time we have achieved some realization on the path of seeing.

Until then, these five views may be very intellectual, and they may be very well researched; we may contemplate them rigorously, but they are still not noble because they are tainted with the ego, and they have the potential to increase our defilements.

Only after we reach the path of seeing, do these views become noble. Now our seeing has the power to defy not only the active destructive emotions but also those latent or "sleeping" destructive emotions. For the first time we will truly understand this first and most important branch of the Noble Eightfold Path, the branch of Right View.

Q & A

Q: Where in the sadhana is the path of seeing?

A: The sadhana is a method of practice, and the path of seeing is based on the individual realizations of the practitioner. After the emptiness mantra in the sadhana, when we generate ourselves as a deity, maybe that could be considered the path of seeing because the preliminary practices are the path of accumulation and the path of application. Due to the power of the path of accumulation and the path of application, we can then see the emptiness by reciting the emptiness mantra, "Om svabhava shuddha sarva dharma svabhava shuddho ham." Out of that emptiness, it is then possible to see oneself as a deity. But this is all still method rather than direct realization.

When we generate a deity out of emptiness, that is objectively supposed to be the path of seeing. But again the path of seeing is not an unconditioned seeing. That's why we have to progress to the next path, the path of meditation, where we have to familiarize ourselves with what we have seen again and again through meditation.

Without any realization, the generation of the deity is just a method of practice. It cannot duplicate the experience. Objectively we have to understand something in the practice, and then subjectively we have to measure where we are on the paths. So those are two separate things.

Objectively we could say that an object appears the same to everyone. Subjectively, however, it could appear very different for different practitioners. Everyone is practicing at a different level.

We may all be practicing the same sadhana; we may all be doing the same visualizations, but without a glimpse of emptiness we may still be on that first path, the path of accumulation of merit. The path of seeing starts from that glimpse of emptiness.

Q: How can I work to break through my fixed ideas and judgements? What if I think people who don't work are lazy? Or what if I judge people for drinking alcohol? Should I go and drink too? How do I work with these assumptions?

A: We must use skillful means and have some understanding of wisdom and compassion. If we know the particular situation and the individual person, then we can determine what will be most helpful.

It depends on our motivation and on seeing how we can help someone. Skillful means are part of the practice of the six paramitas. The six paramitas apply both wisdom and compassion. Even just knowledge and some level of compassion applied together to a situation or circumstance can help to break some of those fixed ideas. Whenever we apply skillful means, a combination of some wisdom and some compassion will arise. Our ability to know specifically what is helpful to an individual depends on what level of awareness and wisdom we have attained.

If a person has some knowledge, but does not have any compassion, then that's one extreme. It may not allow the person to be very helpful. On the other hand, if a person has compassion without any knowledge, that's another extreme and could be equally detrimental. So this is a difficult question to answer.

Helping people, I have noticed, is very hard! Really hard! It's hard in the sense that you may think you are helping someone, but several years may go by and then you find that the approach you were taking was not actually helping that person.

People rarely take responsibility for themselves when things don't work out as they had hoped. They always want to find someone else to blame for their unhappiness. So most of the time they will blame someone who tried to help them! They will say, "Because of you, because of this, now I'm in this situation."

Sometimes we wonder, who are we actually helping? We lack complete wisdom. We don't have complete compassion, so we think maybe we can help in a certain situation, but then there are lots of side effects, see? Doctors, patients, and other professionals know all about this experience! Often what they do to try to help someone creates further complications.

People who have more wisdom and more compassion at least have the confidence that they did their best. Most of the time their efforts will be beneficial, but their actions won't always translate that way. If the intention is pure, then even if the result is not beneficial to the person we are trying to help, at least we are not creating negative karma.

Skillful means, the combination of wisdom and compassion, will help determine what is beneficial to someone for a longer duration and at a deeper level. We will not just be trying to help them on the surface.

Q: Lama, even if we have a very strong belief in karma, it seems that there are situations that present themselves, like an untimely death, that can be challenging to accept. When someone has always been generous and kind it is so difficult to understand why they had a tragic death. And even though there's that understanding of eons of karma accumulating, I'm still wondering if there are ways that we can think about that in order to understand it in our current lives?

A: I think your own practice will be the key. Do lots of accumulation of merit, and do lots of practice. Practice will purify your karma more and more, and then that purification will help you to see things more clearly.

Otherwise, if the practice is not purifying, then no matter how much you will try to see, still your seeing will be shaded with your emotions, and ego, and obscurations, and you will not see clearly.

The best thing is for you to focus on your practice. I think practice will help you to purify your karma, and then you will see karma more clearly.

Until you have purified all your karma, there's no way you will see all the details of karma. I mean you or I can see up to a certain distance with our eyes. That doesn't mean that beyond that sight there are no more objects. How will you believe that Tibet exists somewhere on the top of a mountain? How will you believe, how will you know, if you cannot see it?

If you cannot see Tibet and you cannot travel there, perhaps you will not believe Tibet exists. In a similar way we may ask whether karma exists because we cannot see very far. We have to find a reference. We have to put our faith in the Buddha, as someone who knows. Buddha is the expert on karma.

In our lives I think we give too much importance to the experts.

Sometimes I see in America that we are overtaken by the experts and professionals! For example, because I cannot do everything, and I don't know everything, now, as I face tax season, I have to rely on the accountants. Why do we have to believe them? Because our country is overly regulated, and we don't know all those changes the IRS is making, we think maybe the accountants know better than we do.

If we can rely on tax experts, then why can't we do the same and rely on Buddha for the things we don't yet understand? When you are enlightened, then you have gone beyond time. Going beyond time means seeing past, future, and present all at the same time. That makes the enlightened beings experts on karma!

At our level we can barely see the present and the past. But the more time passes, the longer we live, the less we even remember about the past. Who can remember everything they have learned from elementary school to university? Who can remember what they have done from birth until now?

There's no way, until we purify all karma and destructive emotions, that we will know each and every cause and condition and result of karma. When we don't know, we have to rely on someone who knows, and that is Buddha.

When we put faith in the Buddha, then what Buddha will say is "practice." Buddha has to say that because Buddha wants us to also become Buddha so that we will also know everything.

Buddha gave us teachings to help us practice. Really, that is the purpose. The teachings are not there just to do research on, not to study just for the sake of knowledge. Buddha gave us all these profound teachings to encourage our practice.

Practice is the essence and is the key. It will help you to see eventually, and it will also help you to overcome the mourning of the tragedy which is challenging you right now. By putting faith in the practice you will gain understanding.

Otherwise, if we just keep on asking the question, "Why why why?" then I don't think we will get much of an answer. Only faith will help us to heal. Faith in the Buddha and the resulting faith in our practice.

Chapter Six

The Noble Eightfold Path - Right Intention & Right Speech

Right Intention is the second branch of the Noble Eightfold Path. Intention is very important. Intention in combination with volition is the beginning of all karma and all action. Intention starts in the mind, and then through volition that intention is connected with an object. This is how our intentions become active.

As long as we are in samsara, we have not seen the path of seeing or beyond it. We still struggle with the three root afflictive emotions of desire, anger, and ignorance. Even when we are feeling peaceful and content, those destructive emotions are still "sleeping emotions" in our consciousness. Just because we aren't actively engaged in a destructive emotion doesn't mean that it's not still in our subconscious and able to arise at the slightest provocation. Many of the views we hold in highest esteem are still wrong views when we examine them in depth.

When we investigate this second branch of the Noble Eightfold Path, we realize that sleeping anger resides in us constantly, even when we are not actively experiencing it. Sleeping anger is activated when our wrong intention becomes volition. We direct that anger toward our enemy or toward some object.

Intention has two potentialities. It can be wrong or right, depending on how it arises. Intention is related with mental karma or mental activities, which we call "sems-byung" in Tibetan.

If we look within the mind, we begin to see that the mind has many mental activities. Some scholars translate these activities as emotions. But the Sanskrit word is "chaitta," stemming from the word "chitta" that means mind.

Mind is a general word we use for what is actually a composite of many different activities. These activities can be divided into three categories of positive, negative, and neutral mental activities. In the higher Abhidharma teachings there are fifty-one mental activities described. In the lower Abhidharma there are forty-six mental activities.

Mind is not just one single independent entity. It is composed of many factors. Due to volition, mental activities are activated. Through volition our anger becomes directed to an object that we consider an enemy. When this occurs we may feel like our entire mind is anger. But that anger is also closely related to desire.

Anger arises because there is also an element of desire operating. Maybe that person we don't like, who has now become our enemy, is somehow obstructing our desire and depriving us of what we want. Ignorance is also present in anger. But when the dominant afflictive emotion is anger, we may only recognize that one emotion.

Overcoming anger is one of the primary Right Intentions. There are many spiritual practices designed to help us overcome anger. Developing bodhicitta and loving-kindness can be a great antidote to anger. An angry mind is always activated to harm someone or something through speech or physical actions. Meditations on love and compassion, and especially cultivating bodhicitta, can help us to generate positive emotions towards others.

"Harming" refers to how much physical or mental suffering we create. "Helping" is defined by how much happiness and pleasure we can bring to another being. The Buddhist understanding is that as long as we have love and compassion and bodhicitta, then we are helping others to feel more happiness and to develop the causes of happiness.

On the other hand, when we don't develop these positive qualities, we will continue to experience hate instead of love. We will feel passion instead of compassion. Without the cultivation of bodhicitta, we will experience self-clinging. These negative emotions of hate, passion, and self-clinging create tremendous conflict between ourselves and others.

As long as our egos are not fulfilled, we will want to harm others because they are not letting us have what we want. This is why taking the Bodhisattva vow is so important to our spiritual transformation. The Bodhisattva vow helps us to correct our intention and motivation.

If we don't take a strong resolution such as the Bodhisattva vow, then our intention remains harmful. We may not recognize this because it is so subtle. But if we are attached to ourselves, we will continue to be competitive and to place our own desires above others.

That attachment to the self will extend the territory of the ego further and further into the universe. In some sense, everything becomes a threat to our sense of self. When this egotistical attitude reaches an extreme, we see people in power willing to kill thousands and destroy whole countries in order to extend their territory. This is a magnification of the ego and anger. Buddha gave us practices like bodhicitta to counter these wrong intentions.

Whatever practice we undertake has to start with the mind and mental activities. This is especially true with regard to Right

Intention. When we can overcome our anger in the mind, we can generate Right Intention. Right Intention is the beginning of all wholesome karma. Wrong intention, based on anger, is the root of all harmful activities.

Importance of Taking Precepts and Vows

Taking resolutions and honoring precepts is a vital antidote to wrong intention. Path has a meaning of practice and transformation. Transformation has to take place at the very core. Taking resolutions helps us to correct our motivation on the deepest level.

Most of the time we are not aware of our sleeping emotions. If we are not actively experiencing anger, we may deny that we have any anger at all. But anger still exists silently in our minds. If we take the precept of overcoming any negative actions, this helps us to counteract the roots of that anger in the mind.

The physical and mental precepts we take are disciplines. How quickly these disciplines serve as antidotes to negative emotions depends on the strength of our habitual patterns.

If we are people who are used to expressing anger and being violent, then when we take a precept not to kill, it may be very challenging at first. These habitual patterns of anger are as strong as any other addiction in the mind. If we are addicted to alcohol or drugs, then when we make resolutions to quit those addictions, it will be extremely challenging in the beginning.

In the case of alcohol, repeated intoxication has created a systemic dependency. When we first deprive the body of this substance, it may be very uncomfortable. Even if we try to detox from caffeine, the withdrawal may give us a terrible headache and make us exhausted.

The discomfort of detox is a result of how these substances have become part of our entire physical bodies. In a similar way, when we first try to overcome the destructive emotion of anger, we may be surprised by the strength of that habitual pattern. It is very difficult to begin cleansing our minds of that addiction.

Overcoming Anger, Desire, and Ignorance

When we operate in certain ways for years and years, our habitual patterns become so strong that we mistake them for our personalities. We may start to believe that we are wired to have a short temper. We may claim that we are just emotional and passionate by nature.

If we do anything with enough repetition, we begin to believe it is a fixed personality trait. These negative habitual patterns become mental addictions very easily. We begin to believe that this is who we are by nature and that it is not in our control to change.

Most of the Buddhist precepts we take, are to counteract these patterns of thought and action. In the beginning this may feel like a very artificial repression of emotion, but eventually these antidotes will begin to break down the roots of even our sleeping emotions.

Although our experience of active anger may seem the most challenging to overcome, it is actually the subtle sleeping anger which is hardest to uproot. Active anger exists because, in the first place, we have this sleeping aggression deep down in our minds. When we can begin to access these more subtle levels of emotion, we can break down the root causes of this anger.

It is vital that we honor our precepts and vows. This discipline is essential to the work of deep transformation. Overcoming anger is a vital component of Right Intention.

The other very important aspect of cultivating Right Intention is overcoming desire. As we have discussed, anger and desire are very dependent on each other. We become angry when our desire is not fulfilled. When we don't get something we want, or when something threatens our egos, we have pain and anger. These emotions are all mixed together.

As long as we have sleeping ignorance, we will also be subject to all five of the wrong views we discussed in the previous chapter. Although ignorance is the most difficult sleeping emotion to recognize because it is so subtle, it is still considered a primary cause.

Overcoming ignorance is also included in Right Intention. When we take precepts, we are correcting three unwholesome or non-virtuous mental actions. The first is coveting, which is related to desire. The second is a harming mind, which is related to anger. The third is wrong view which is related to ignorance. These are the three fundamental wrong intentions that the precepts aim to correct.

This second branch of the Noble Eightfold Path is primarily concerned with ways to overcome the harmful mind of anger and its corresponding emotion of desire. Overcoming desire is central, especially because we humans are living in the desire realm, and everything we consume is based on attachment.

If we examine all our feelings of happiness and pleasure, we realize we are often operating with a very conflicting message here in the desire realm. We may say that we act virtuously in order to have happiness and pleasure, but even that intention is not pure. It is still very relative. That happiness and pleasure seeking is still rooted in feelings of desire and self-clinging.

The Importance of Renunciation

If our virtuous activities are focused on attaining happiness and pleasure, then that result is not perfect. When we look closely, we see that pleasure always becomes the cause of future desire. Since that pleasure is not permanent, the minute it fades we have a strong desire to experience it again.

Momentary happiness becomes the cause and condition of more desire. The more we consume, the more our appetite grows here in the desire realm. This is the reason why the resolution of renunciation is so strongly emphasized in Buddhist practice. Renunciation is key to overcoming our desires.

In the graduated path, whether it is in the Hinayana, Mahayana, or Vajrayana Buddhist practices, renunciation is essential. Why is renunciation so important? Because renunciation is our first step in gaining some freedom from desire.

If we examine all the vows, from the first precept we take of not killing, right up to the full ordination vows which include some two hundred and fifty precepts, we can understand why the Buddha developed such complex ethics of renunciation. Renunciation is the essential method to counteract desire.

Desire creates many challenges in our meditation practice. The moment we want to focus on one object of meditation, then it seems a desirable object immediately shows up in our minds instead.

When our desire is not fulfilled, we become angry or irritable. Desire obscures our ability to see reality clearly. As long as we have desire, we never see the true nature of an object. We will romanticize one object; we will reject another object. We will bring all these conflicting emotions into our meditation practices, and they will obscure our vision.

Cultivating renunciation is essential in our practice. This is the reason why we take all these precepts. The precepts are presented in terms of renunciation: no killing, no stealing etc. We are trying to stay away from those activities. We are trying to refrain from those actions and those emotions. Once we have taken the precepts, then each time we refrain from a negative activity, we are actually cultivating positive qualities.

If we are used to doing something all the time, like drinking or smoking, then abstaining will be very difficult. Right Intention begins with renunciation. If we are on the Mahayana path, then we also take the Bodhisattva vow and cultivate love and compassion for the sake of all sentient beings.

Right Intention and Karma

Right Intention is so important because it is the beginning of all karma. Karma is multidimensional and very complex. Karma starts with our intention and volition. If we change our intention, then we begin to transform our karma.

For a yogi who has reached the path of seeing, the intention is noble because it is free from both anger and desire. At this point the yogi has seen the wisdom. Once we have seen wisdom, we have overcome ignorance, and most actions will become noble.

Right now our actions are not noble because our intentions are shaded by ignorance. If we examine the five wrong views closely and reflect on our own personal views, we will begin to see that what we thought were right views are actually still arising from ignorance.

Right View and Right Intention, as a practice, help us to overcome all the root mental negativities of ignorance, anger, and desire. Ignorance by itself, anger by itself, and desire by itself are not karma. But when they are drawn towards an object by intention and volition in the mind, they become action. This action is harmful when it is rooted in the afflictive emotions and then it becomes part of our karma.

We need to make the distinction between emotions and actions. It is important to examine them separately, as well as to look at what happens when they are combined. Buddha's teachings help us to better understand how and why we are acting and feeling in certain ways.

Often, when we do things, we limit our actions only to the verbal and the physical levels of expression. We usually don't look deeper to see the roots of our intentions. Intentions are often overwhelming and blinding to us. Intention is the root of action. When defilements and emotions are directed toward objects by volition, then they become karma.

These first two branches of the Noble Eightfold Path are related to mental actions. They describe the right mental actions and offer insight into overcoming wrong mental actions. Buddhist practice involves taking vows and precepts to counteract the destructive emotions and their causes.

Right Speech

The third branch of the Noble Eightfold Path is Right Speech. In order to understand Right Speech, we have to learn how to overcome wrong speech. Buddha taught four categories of wrong speech.

Idle Chatter

The first category is idle talk. This means useless trivial chatter without much meaning. This chatter arises from unfiltered thoughts and concepts. If we have a lot of inner chattering inside our own minds, we may feel the need to express it verbally. This expression may give us some relief.

Some psychologists at Harvard conducted a study. They determined that talking on the phone makes people happier. Maybe this happiness is due to the fact that when we are talking we forget about ourselves. Maybe this distraction makes us feel better.

But trivial conversations don't do anything fundamentally transformative. Useless chatter is like watching an entertaining movie. It's just another way of trying to forget or deny other feelings by distracting ourselves. So while it may be temporarily enjoyable, idle conversation is actually a waste of our energy.

Buddha preferred to do meditation. Buddha maintained a noble silence. That's why Buddha's name was "Shakyamuni. "Muni" means "silent one."

Generally we meditate in silence because it helps to quiet the chattering inside us. Talking activates certain parts of the brain that may not be conducive to meditation. Even if we talk a lot during times when we are not practicing, this could still have a lasting effect on the quality of our minds.

Idle talk is considered wrong speech because it is just a waste of our effort. Useless chatter becomes the source of lots of emotions and concepts. Often we speak before we think, and this can be harmful to others. Talking gets us into lots of trouble! Talking also includes so much affirming and negating that we are led into extremes of thinking.

There is a story of the Buddha that illustrates this point. Once some hunters were chasing a deer, and they came upon the Buddha. They asked Buddha where the deer went. Buddha maintained his noble silence. If he mentioned the truth of where the deer went, then the hunters would kill the deer. But he also could not lie. By maintaining silence he avoided creating any negative karma.

Another example is the very famous Fourteen Questions which Buddha didn't answer. Now this is not necessarily because Buddha didn't know the answers. It has more to do with the fact that Buddha knew that regardless of whether he answered "yes" or "no," he could somehow mislead the questioner toward a wrong conclusion.

Talking gives rise to many emotions in ourselves and in others. If we can try to talk less and less, and maintain that noble silence, we will experience more peace.

In order to counteract this form of wrong speech, we can strive to have meaningful conversations and to only speak when it is necessary and useful. We can choose silence instead of trivial chatter.

Lying

Lying is another form of wrong speech. The obvious antidote to lying is to always tell the truth. But karma is still in the realm of relativity. It is not a perfection. For this reason there are exceptions where telling the truth can be too harmful.

Only when we are like Buddha, and we know everything, will

we know what is truly helpful. If lying brings pain and suffering, then we must counteract that by telling the truth.

Harsh Speech and Deceptive Speech

A third action we must avoid is harsh speech. Buddha always emphasized speaking gently. Speaking harshly actually increases anger, and it can be very harmful to others. Speaking gently is very important to maintaining Right Speech.

The fourth action to avoid is speaking deceptively. Deception here has a meaning of misleading others. We may inflate some story in order to benefit ourselves. Saying things with the intention of personal gain, whether it's fame, power, attention, or wealth, is all considered deceptive speech.

Right Speech and the Ten Non-Virtues

The path of Right Speech helps us to overcome all the negative karma that is motivated by destructive emotions. Right Speech means avoiding all of those four types of wrong speech. Those four types of wrong speech are included in the natural law of the ten non-virtues.

The ten non-virtues include three mental non-virtues, three physical non-virtues, and the four verbal non-virtues we have just discussed. The fact that speech has the most non-virtues attached to it is a reflection of how much karma is produced by our verbal actions. Our karma is primarily created through our speech.

The extent to which physical actions affect others is fairly limited. It is limited because the target of those physical actions has to be close by to feel the effects. Speech can reach much further than physical actions, and as a result it can create so much more karma.

We can call someone who lives in India on the telephone, and we can yell at them or lie. We can be deceptive or speak harshly. But it's hard for us to hit someone in India from here! Speech, however, is very powerful. So that's why there are four non-virtues that involve speech.

We need to maintain Right Speech for as long as we can. The more meditation we do, and the more we maintain a noble silence, the better chance there is that all four negative aspects of speech can be overcome. Most of our social interactions are based on speech. The more we can pray or chant or meditate, the more we can counteract these four aspects of wrong speech.

We have now discussed the first three branches of the Noble Eightfold Path. These include Right View, Right Intention, and Right Speech. As a result we have covered all the wrong actions related with mind and all the wrong actions related with speech.

Q & A

Q: Lama, how do we know when to renounce, especially say an object of desire, or when to incorporate the energy created by that towards our practice of wisdom? For example, I love dark chocolate. I could completely avoid ever getting dark chocolate again if I like, but then I might just think about it every day. Or I could get a chocolate bar and eat half of it, and put the remainder on my dashboard, and think about it for the whole rest of my drive. Or I could do what I do now, which is to buy the chocolate bar and eat the whole thing. At what point do you know when to completely avoid something or when to incorporate it into your practice?

A: Our goal is to overcome desire, to overcome ignorance, and to overcome anger. But how much can we do? We have to be practical. We cannot try to do more than we are capable of.

If we have lots of desire, and then we try to give something up completely overnight, I don't think that will be very healthy. Buddha himself has said we have to practice according to our level.

If we give something up completely, and still we are at peace, then maybe we were ready for that. But if giving something up completely makes us miserable, then at some point we might even give up on our spiritual practice! That outcome would be very counterproductive, but it is one of the risks of practicing beyond our level.

Buddha taught a general objective practice, discipline, and training. Subjectively, personally, then, we have to practice in a way that is most helpful to us. Although renunciation is strongly emphasized in the Hinayana tradition, it is not as emphasized in the Mahayana and Vajrayana traditions. Vajrayana is actually quite the opposite. Vajrayana has more to do with incorporating desire, with using everything for our transformation instead of renouncing it.

So the tantric way might be, not to renounce it, but to eat lots of chocolate instead! Then we will know what eating chocolate is. It is human nature to want what we are told we cannot have. Whenever I've seen parents saying, "no, no, no," to their kids, it seems the kids always rebel and want even more strongly what is being denied to them!

One of my relatives said that when he lived in Nepal, when his kids would come home from school, they always liked to eat oranges. If he gave one orange to each child, the children always wanted more. But if he bought lots of oranges and just put them on the table, his children would ignore them! They only wanted oranges when they couldn't have many.

So there is a sense organ level of consumption, but there is also an emotional level. The emotional level is apparent whenever we feel denied or deprived and then want to have more of something.

Most things that we are deprived of we will start to crave. Our nature is rebellious that way. Now, if we are strong enough, then even if we eat whatever we want, we will still not get addicted. In that case, instead of the experience of eating a whole chocolate bar making us momentarily satisfied, we may instead overcome the emotions related to the chocolate altogether. Then that's tantra.

I think the practice is all very subjective, based on where we are. But objectively, Buddha gave these teachings because there are many different kinds of practitioners. So I don't have a proper answer for you. I think you have to find out for yourself.

Q: If one is having a negative emotion, and there's an object, but one does not act, that emotion is not karma?

A: Yes, the emotion itself is not karma. Volition has the power to aim the intention toward the object, to cause an action of some type. So volition is the beginning of all the mental actions. That is what creates karma.

Q: Lama, if an emotion with an intention behind it doesn't become volition or action, would that still generate karma?

A: The kind of intention I'm referring to here is only within the context of the Noble Eightfold Path. Sometimes intention has a second meaning. In Tibetan, the second meaning is called "dun pa." People can translate this as "interest," interest in the sense that when we have anger, such anger becomes interested in killing. That volition is the mental activity which aims the emotions toward some object. Tell me your question again?

Q: I'm just wondering if the intention alone, without action, is still producing karma?

A: If we say anger is the intention, then with anger as the intention, there's no volition yet. If, on the other hand, you're angry toward an enemy, then that anger has intention as well as volition, and even if you don't act, that volition does have karma.

Q: So this includes harming yourself through anger?

A: Yes, it's the same. You have anger, and with that anger if you harm your physical body, it's the same karma as if you harm an enemy. You are now the object of that anger. I mean right now, as people, we think that our minds and our bodies are the same thing. But if we go deeper, we learn that mind and body are different. They can become subject and object.

Q: Lama, what if you kill without anger, you cause an action without the three poisons? Would the karma be different?

A: That is possible. When doctors do surgery, they don't want to harm a patient. But a patient can still end up dying as a result of surgery. I don't think that's a wrong action. If the doctors have done their very best and have worked with lots of love and compassion, maybe it is considered a good action regardless of the outcome. Or if the doctors don't have any emotions at all, then that's a neutral karma. The karma related to killing is dependent on the emotions. It can be neutral karma; it can be positive karma; it can also be negative.

There are stories of some of the eighty-four Mahasiddhas, those great Indian yogis, killing fish. Maybe they killed fish, but they didn't have any emotions. They acted out of wisdom, out of emptiness. So they are free from karma. There's neither positive nor negative karma; there's not even neutral karma. They've gone beyond everything. If they are fishing out of emptiness and wisdom, there's no fish, no fisherman, and there is no karma of killing.

This is how it is when you are an enlightened being. You have gone beyond karma. So someone who is enlightened may seem to be killing something, but personally for them, maybe it is beyond killing. So I think it is very subjective. It is dependent upon what state of mind we do things in. I think even in our case, we do many killings just based on neutral karma. We kill so many small insects and such by accident, without even knowing.

Q: Say a person has a destructive emotion and there is an object, but there is no volition or action. If the person is monitoring his or her mind, emotions, and thoughts and choosing not to act, can that be considered an antidote that has been applied?

A: Can you give me an example?

Q: Someone does something to you, and you feel angry. Rather than using wrong speech or negative action, you just say "I'm angry" and just use silence and right speech. Is that an antidote being applied? What is that?

A: The main purpose of all this Right Action is to overcome anger - both the active anger and the sleeping anger. So once we get angry at someone, actually, there's a little bit of volition, and there's emotion. So although it's not harming the other person, it is still harming us. Because the moment we express such anger, even in our own minds, our anger becomes stronger. By becoming angry, we strengthen our habitual pattern of anger.

That's why both repression and expression can strengthen an emotion. In Buddhist practice, going beyond both repression and expression is important. The ideal antidote is arrived at through meditation. It is arrived at when you have mindfulness and are aware of your anger, but you still don't express or repress your anger at all. When you express and when you repress, I think either way you are still strengthening the anger.

Chapter Seven
The Noble Eightfold Path - Right Action & Right Livelihood

The fourth branch of the Noble Eightfold Path is Right Action. When we refer to an action such as killing, this includes not only the killing of humans, but also the killing of any other sentient beings, even the smallest insect.

As a society we presume killing always has to do with anger. But the fact is, we probably kill more from desire and ignorance. We've created an entire meat industry out of our desire for certain foods. Back in the primitive world, we would hunt for just enough food to feed ourselves, but the modern world is very different.

Once I met one of the executors working at a Tyson Chicken slaughterhouse. He told me that every day they kill millions of chickens. When the market was opened to China, the killing greatly multiplied. They exported lots of chicken meat to China. When we watch documentaries on the food industry, then we understand that this era's killing has extended far beyond what it once was. Today we have corporate industrialized killing of great numbers of sentient beings.

One of my Lama friends from New York sent me a video of how pigs are raised and traded. It would be hard to eat pork ever again after watching that suffering. When we sit down to eat at our tables, we rarely think of where the meat comes from and of how inhumane the conditions were for those poor, abused animals.

Right Action is not just about action related to humans. Right

Action is also about how we treat animals and other beings. We kill many beings through our desire and ignorance.

Right Action has to do with overcoming our wrong actions with regard to other humans, as well as to all other sentient beings. These wrong actions, such as killing, can arise from any or all of the three destructive emotions of desire, anger, and ignorance. But regardless of which destructive emotions are involved, killing is wrong as far as karmic law is concerned. Karmic law has nothing to do with the laws of a particular country.

Even within Buddhism, depending on our practice and on how many precepts we have taken, there are different consequences. But as far as natural law is concerned, any actions we do based on the destructive emotions are considered wrong actions.

Wrong action is not just related with other sentient beings. Wrong actions can also be related to things. For example, a wrong action would be to misuse something which is not ours. It is even possible to commit wrong actions with objects which we possess.

Right Action involves finding some kind of middle path. Buddha's life is a good example of finding a middle path. For six years Buddha lived as an ascetic. He starved himself and meditated. But this strict discipline and deprivation did not allow for very high realization. At the end of his sixth year, a girl from the nearby village offered him some rice pudding. When Buddha tasted the rice pudding his meditation experience became stronger. In this moment he recognized that it is better to maintain a middle way on the spiritual path.

We cannot become too extreme in our actions. Even if we own something, we should be careful not to misuse it. Most actions are expressions of emotion. If our expressions serve to increase our destructive emotions, we need to change how we relate to an object. If we deprive ourselves of something, and if our minds are not strong, then this can increase our pain and generate more anger.

Deprivation can create many emotions for people who are poor. If you do not have many material things, if your basic needs are not being met, then deep down you can carry resentment towards those who are wealthy. We see these class struggles throughout history.

On the other hand, if we are indulging too much, then that indulgence can make us more narcissistic. Our appetites can become insatiable. We are always craving more. Neither extreme will bring us into the middle way.

This fourth branch of the Noble Eightfold Path shows us that whatever action increases our destructive emotions is potentially a wrong action. And whatever actions help us to overcome our destructive emotions will have the potential of increasing positive things.

How we own things and what we own are also part of Right Action. This is very controversial. As a developed society, we have developed a sense of entitlement based on artificial systems. These systems don't have any intrinsic value. The value is only projected.

The only intrinsic value is what is directly related to sustaining our lives. We place a great deal of importance on money, as if that alone were keeping us alive. But without air, without earth, or water, or energy, or soil, money would be worthless. Money does not actually keep us alive. If we cannot breathe, then no matter how much money we have, we cannot live. But our entire society is based on artificial projections of value. Society has convinced us that we need many things.

The former prime minister of Malaysia, Dr. Mahathir, is a great economist. Recently I watched an interview with him on the BBC. He said that our present economic system is really just high stakes gambling. The stock market probably deals with billions of dollars every day, but really nothing is getting produced through the stock exchange. Traders are buying and selling billions of dollars, but there is nothing tangible to show for this. It's all just numbers and projected values.

Dr Mahathir said that as long as we keep on doing this, our economy will always be at risk. It's all just legalized gambling. He suggested that everyone who is trading like that needs to produce something instead. Then, according to what is produced, they should get a return. They can live on such a return. Otherwise, if we try to live based on gambling monies, then someday we may lose everything. We have already seen Wall Street suffer major losses in the past.

This leads us to the topic of stealing. If we look into it more deeply, we come to understand that whatever we use that we don't own, is actually a form of stealing. Even if we own something but we misuse is it and waste it, then in some sense we are depriving others of these resources. With every liter of gas we use, we are essentially taking the earth's energy.

If we look closely at our consumption of objects, it is important to connect that consumption with cultivating positive emotions. Every time we eat food, we should bring some purpose to why we are eating.

In Buddhist food offering prayers it says very clearly, "I'm not eating this food out of desire, out of anger, out of ego or pride. I'm eating just to sustain my physical body with the essence and nutrients my body requires, so that I can do practice and positive deeds."

We should learn to approach everything we do in our lives with this clarity of purpose. If we have altruistic goals, then there is more justification for our use of resources. Otherwise, if we are living just to eat, then what is the difference between humans and animals?

Sakya Pandita said in his Elegant Sayings that wild animals spend their whole day looking for something to eat. They are just focused on basic survival. So what is the difference between animals and humans? There is no difference if we too are living only to consume. But if we live so that we can do something beneficial for ourselves and others, then we are engaging in Right Action. Right Action includes our attitude toward all the things we consume.

Another important aspect of Right Action is how we act in our interpersonal relationships. How we conduct ourselves with regard to others is incredibly important. If our relationships are based on strong destructive emotions like anger and desire, then we can become obsessed or aggressive. Good relationships depend on how many positive qualities of mind we bring to one another. Qualities such as love, compassion, and forgiveness have far more potential to create and sustain positive relationships.

Right Action includes all of the physical actions. We try to bring some positive emotions and awareness into everything we engage with through our senses. Whether it's what we look at, what we hear, what we smell, or what we eat, we try to bring some positive qualities to this experience. In essence, Right Action has to do with how we conduct ourselves physically in relation to all sentient beings and to all objects.

Right Livelihood

The fifth branch of the Noble Eightfold Path is Right Livelihood. Buddha specifically described four wrong livelihoods.

The first wrong livelihood is selling intoxicants like alcohol or drugs because these increase our ignorance. Intoxication can deprive people of their mindfulness, their attention, and their conscious discrimination of what is right and wrong. For this reason, selling intoxicants is actually one of the most dangerous livelihoods.

I am not sure why people drink so much. Sometimes when people are depressed they drink. Sometimes it seems like a cultural thing. Cultures can promote drinking as a part of the social fabric. In Tibet they drink this home-brewed drink called "chang." For many, chang is a source of enjoyment and festivity to celebrate together or to forget their pain and suffering. But slowly it becomes the cause of many other problems, and we see an increase in addiction.

Drugs are also very detrimental. Engaging in selling drugs is a wrong livelihood because drugs completely cloud a person's mind. Drug users lose the ability to discriminate between what is right and what is wrong. There are many drug induced crimes.

The second wrong livelihood Buddha described is that of being a butcher. Any worker in a modern slaughterhouse could be said to have wrong livelihood. The more meat eaters there are, the greater the demand for meat will be. We essentially create more killers.

Killing is taking another life forcefully. Due to that unnatural death there is so much pain. Why does someone become a butcher, and why does that person kill? There is desire involved, even if it's just for material gain, just for a paycheck. Killing of animals or any sentient beings is very heavy karma.

The third wrong livelihood that Buddha described is dealing in the manufacture and sale of weapons. In Buddha's time maybe that just pertained to bows and arrows and cruder weapons. These days weapons have become massively destructive. Nuclear bombs have the potential to destroy the planet, so dealing in weapons is very destructive. It creates lethal karma by inflicting so much pain and suffering.

The fourth wrong livelihood Buddha described was the trafficking of humans, whether in a slave trade, or for prostitution, or for any kind of human rights abuse. This produces incredibly heavy karma as well.

Right Livelihood should be something that is ethical, humane, and that cultivates more positive qualities within us and within others. Any livelihood which cultivates more destructive emotions in ourselves and others is considered wrong.

Now there are also more subtle types of wrong livelihood. Teachers, for example, have to be very careful. My teacher used to say, "If you become a teacher and a faith object, then people will make offerings to you. If you misuse those offerings then that's a very heavy karma."

Buddha said in the Sutras, "If people offer something to you out of faith, and you misuse the offering, that is such heavy karma to digest that you will need steel teeth to chew those offerings!"

Any livelihood we have which is beneficial for us and beneficial for others is Right Livelihood. Whenever a livelihood becomes harmful to oneself and others, then that is a wrong livelihood. These are some aspects that we who are on the spiritual path have to attend to very carefully.

Generally, in Buddhist understanding, as long as we are more harmonious with the natural law of karma, that harmonious living will bring more harmony with nature, and as a result there will be more peace.

Many of these aspects, even in the way we live, are regulated by government statutes. These statutes are not necessarily always ethical, but most of the time the natural laws are incorporated into the state and federal laws. So generally we will need to follow the laws unless they openly oppose our spiritual ethical vows and precepts.

Taking precepts is not necessarily imposed on us to force us to do something good. Taking precepts is a way of creating very good ethical protection through natural laws. As a by-product, these can offer us protection from legal laws. For example, drinking may be legal here, but driving drunk is highly illegal. Through our precepts of refraining from drinking, we automatically protect ourselves from breaking the laws against drunk driving.

Even though we take the precepts, we are still human, and sometimes we make mistakes. However, we have many confessional and purification practices to correct our motivation and renew our vows.

There are general confession practices, and in the higher teachings we have Vajrasattva purification practices. It is always better to take the precepts, even if we sometimes make mistakes. It's better that we make the resolution to become stronger, even if we sometimes fail along the way and need to recommit ourselves.

Taking precepts is important and beneficial. Taking the precepts helps us to have better actions. All of the Pratimoksha vows are designed as antidotes and guidelines. Right View and Right Intention are related with mental action. Right Speech is related with verbal action. Right Action and Right Livelihood are related with physical action.

The Noble Eightfold Path has been perfected by those noble yogis who have seen the path of seeing. We are not at that level yet. We still need to admit that we have many wrong views, wrong intentions, wrong actions, and wrong habits of speech, and then we have to apply the antidotes for how to correct them. Taking the vows and making positive resolutions are fundamental to creating this transformation.

Q & A

Q: Lama, I've noticed that after a while the vows seem to gradually erode away potentials for negativities to occur. It is almost as if they have some kind of force in themselves when they are applied. For example, let's say about not taking intoxicants. In my life I have little time to go out carousing. I was told that the desire to be intoxicated is not the same as having a drink in company, yet I have found that even my desire for having a drink in company has dropped away. So now it's less about trying to live up to a vow, but rather that the desire has simply dropped. Can you comment on that?

A: That's correct. For example, killing has multiple results. The more you kill, the more you want to kill. This is called "the result similar to the action." That's how habitual patterns are formed in you. At some point killing becomes part of your personality. Maybe you don't even feel anything when you kill someone.

Once my Lama friend told me a story about a warrior he had met. The warrior showed this Lama a knife. The warrior said, "I have killed many people with this knife." So my friend said, "How do you feel when killing?" The warrior said that the first time he killed someone it was very difficult and he felt scared and emotional. But after killing many people, he said he didn't feel anything anymore. He became a coldhearted murderer and he didn't care or feel anything. It became so easy to kill because he had gotten so used to it.

Now, on the other hand, when we take a vow not to kill, this vow also has multiple results. Here too there is a result similar to the action. By not killing again and again, then we don't have that urge or desire. That is one of the results that the vows have strengthened. This can apply to any karma. In this way we change the deeper habitual patterns and our personalities.

With regard to intoxication: drugs and alcohol are so common. If people become intoxicated on a regular basis, the toxins become part of their cells. Once people become addicted, they may need a drink the moment they wake up. Otherwise they may be shaking and unable to function. After detoxing they may start to feel a little bit better. Then if they can continue to stay sober, at some point every cell in their bodies will become free from craving that chemical.

This is how addiction manifests at the physical level. But all of these addictions have their origin at a deeper emotional level. So if we take a very strong vow at the level of the mind and emotion, then that resolution has the power to overcome many physical weaknesses.

If we can take the vows on both the physical and mental levels, the results will be stronger. The vows are mostly dealing with refraining from a thought or action. Most of the physical and verbal resolutions are related to not doing certain things. Because these habitual patterns are so ingrained in us, we have to apply an antidote to stop them. When that is successful, we begin to see the results.

Q: Lama, when we are talking about the six paramitas, we say that a difference between a normal action and one that is considered a paramita or a "perfection" is the ingredient of wisdom. Take generosity for instance. When somebody understands the emptiness of the three spheres, that there is emptiness in the giver, the receiver, and the gift, then that understanding makes a great difference in terms of the act of generosity. That wisdom of seeing the emptiness, makes it a perfection. So I was wondering if that same understanding plays a role in Right Action or Right View for example?

A: I think when you are referring to that kind of perfection, then it has gone beyond both right and wrong. That's why it is considered a perfection. Right and wrong are still interdependent. As long as there is right and wrong, then there is no perfection. Perfection is the highest level. At the level of perfection there is no karma.

Here we are talking about good and bad karma. Right is good karma, and wrong is bad karma. When we have lots of wrong karma, the first thing we can do is take vows to correct that karma. It would be very difficult to jump from a place of negative karma to a perfection.

I think all right actions are basically a bridge between doing things that are wrong and gaining a state of perfection. At the level of perfection we will have gone beyond karma entirely. Right and wrong are still relative. Perfection is ultimate.

Q: Lama, so you can drink, once you've gone beyond?

A: Or maybe you can drink, and you don't get drunk. I'm just kidding! Because your drink is emptiness! That's what we are actually trying to do with Tsog offerings and all the highest level of inner offerings when we offer alcohol and meat. At first we purify them into emptiness. We bless them by saying, "Om svabhava shuddha sarva dharma svabhava shuddho ham." We transform them into emptiness. Then those substances become the same. Whether it's meat or alcohol or whatever, we purify them all into emptiness.

In these Tsog rituals, we offer the objects we consume that ordinarily increase our defilements. In our worldly life, we think that whenever we want to have a good party or enjoy ourselves we have to have drinks and all kinds of delicious meat and food because we are used to enjoying them.

Now when we purify these same enjoyments into emptiness, with the power of mantra, mudra, and meditation, then out of emptiness we generate them as nectar.

The Mahasiddha Virupa could do this. Once, when he was traveling, he entered a tavern at an inn. He drank all of their beer, and still he didn't get drunk. This was because he had achieved a very high level of realization. Those drinks did not in any way actually intoxicate him. Instead they increased his wisdom and compassion.

But to do what Virupa did, we need to have a high level of realization. We need to have a system which can transform those defilements. Otherwise it can be risky. If we are not ready to make poison into medicine, then it can be dangerous. Until then, if we have not seen emptiness, then we should think twice before we drink. Previously, many of our yoga students also took vows. I gave people a choice of how many vows they wished to take. Many people took the vow of not killing for their whole lives, but most people had a problem with taking the vow of not drinking.

If we keep on drinking, and we get drunk, then there's a real danger of destroying all our other vows too! Still I think it's better to take the vows even though we make mistakes. We can make confessions, and then we can take the vows again. That is better than not taking the vows at all.

Chapter Eight

The Noble Eightfold Path - Right Effort

Right Effort is the sixth branch of the Noble Eightfold Path. Right Effort can also be translated as Right Diligence. To know this noble path we have to reflect back upon all the previous five noble paths. Right Effort is about integrating all those other noble paths into our lives.

This was also true of the first noble path of Right View. We have to know what all the wrong views are in order to understand what Right View means. In a similar way, it is important to understand all the other paths in order to practice Right Effort.

As we have discussed, Right View and Right Intention are related more with mental actions and mental karmas. Right View is very connected to Right Intention because our view effects all our thoughts. Intention starts in the mind.

The Three Wrong Mental Karmas

There are three wrong mental karmas: wrong views, the harming mind, and coveting. Those are related with the three fundamental destructive emotions of ignorance, desire and anger.

Ignorance is related to wrong views. Even if we have cultivated lots of intellectual ideas, if our conclusions are wrong, they are still part of ignorance. Desire and anger are related to wrong intentions. A state of mind that is desirous, harmful, or coveting, is arising from wrong thoughts or mental actions. When we are free from these three destructive emotions, we will have Right View and Right Intention.

Right Effort

In contemplating Right Effort, it is important to remember all the aspects of wrong speech: lying, idle chatter, and harsh words. We must also remember all the wrong actions and the wrong livelihoods.

Right Effort means increasing our right activities on all three levels: mentally, verbally, and physically. We increase our Right Effort at the mental level when we cultivate all the right thoughts. We increase our Right Effort at the verbal level when we strive to cultivate right speech, and we act with Right Effort at the physical level when we perform all the right deeds.

The Sanskrit word for "Right Effort" is "virya." Virya is part of the practice of the six perfections, and it has a deeper meaning. It implies that enthusiasm for wholesome activities is considered Right Effort. Whenever we engage diligently in positive activities, we help to free ourselves at the mental, verbal, and physical levels.

Right Effort is essential to the process of transformation. This happens at a very individual level. Whether we will enjoy wholesome activities is dependent upon our habitual patterns. If we have been enjoying all the wrong activities, then we have created habits that are very hard to break.

For example, if someone has become a pathological liar, it will be very difficult for that person to say something truthful. Or when people have engaged in killing for long periods of time, they can become very cold hearted. They may not even feel anything when they kill.

These negative patterns become entrenched in us. How long have we been thinking certain thoughts? How are we accustomed to speaking, and what are our physical tendencies? According to these habitual patterns, our personalities will be formed. At a certain point we may even believe that these personalities are our true natures. When we first try to counteract these tendencies, it may be very challenging and stressful.

For example, the first time we do meditation it can be physically and mentally painful! Our minds are not used to a meditative state. We are met with a waterfall of chattering thoughts and feelings. Our bodies may be very restless and uncomfortable when we first try to sit still. In order to transform ourselves though, we need to begin with this right effort.

How do we cultivate the energy to meditate? Most of our enthusiasm is cultivated based on what we enjoy doing. If we like doing something, we will sacrifice everything to pursue it. We may even risk our lives to get to the top of the Himalayas or to travel deep into the oceans, and yet it may be very difficult to cultivate an interest in meditation.

How do we create the energy to do wholesome things? This is our challenge. If we are used to doing all the unwholesome activities, engaging in wrong speech and negative deeds, then how can we make that shift?

Meeting a teacher is critical to beginning that transformation. We have to meet a guru or mentor with whom we feel a strong connection. Or perhaps we will feel drawn to a temple or deeply inspired by a teaching. Something has to happen to activate our effort. Buddhists call this a "karmic connection." That is where our spiritual journey begins.

The Power of Faith

Buddha said there are five powers, and the first power is faith. When we have faith, it can generate more effort. Effort is the second power.

We can see this among yogis and meditators. Those who have strong faith can recite mantras all day long, or even meditate in a small cave for years. In the beginning, faith might not be based on any knowledge or wisdom. It may just be blind faith similar to when we fall in love with someone, but it has the power to increase our effort.

When we first fall in love with someone, we may think about that person constantly. Our feelings are very powerful, and we may even lose ourselves in that love. That feeling of falling in love is very similar to that first feeling of blind faith. The only difference is that on the spiritual path, the object of our love is pure. For this reason it becomes faith, rather than worldly romantic love or attachment. When we fall in love with the Dharma, when we fall in love with Buddha, when we become devoted to our gurus, then that love becomes faith.

That karmic connection to the teacher or to the Dharma is very important. In the beginning we might not know who Buddha is or what the teachings are about. Maybe we don't have any meditation experience. But if we feel a strong connection to a teacher, it will generate effort.

If we have not made such a connection, then how will we be inspired to pursue the teachings? Karmic connection, or whatever term we prefer to use for that feeling of inspiration, is the beginning of cultivating our effort. Only when we meet a spiritual person, or when we go through a life changing event, will we pay attention and pursue the teachings. Otherwise it is difficult to break out of our habitual patterns.

The more we pursue the teachings, the more interest and attention we will have. As we cultivate a relationship to a spiritual teacher, we will study that teacher's actions, and we will investigate the truths of the teachings.

If the truth resonates in us, and if we trust that we have met a true teacher, then we will begin to emulate these spiritual qualities. However, as our blind faith wears off, if we discover that we do not trust this path or this teacher, we will break away from this relationship.

If our faith remains strong, it deepens our effort. Through meditation and study we will begin to know more about the Buddha, the Dharma, and the Sangha. The more we learn about these truths and qualities, the more we aspire to find these qualities in ourselves.

This is the stage where our "blind faith" becomes "unshakeable faith." At this stage we have tested the methods. We have observed the teacher for a period of time. We have used our brains as well as our hearts. Now our emotions of faith and our intellectual reason have come together to give us real conviction.

When faith and reason are combined they produce an unshakeable faith. Unshakeable faith helps us to have Right Effort. We begin to completely devote our lives to wholesome activities of body, speech, and mind.

Now, unshakeable faith doesn't mean that we are perfect. We may still have many imperfections, but the strength of our faith begins to transform our lives on every level. At this stage, no matter what happens, nothing will turn us away from our faith in the teachings.

Until our faith is unshakeable, we are operating on blind faith that is based on feelings. Our feelings and circumstances are changing constantly. That's why we are so fickle in so many environments and relationships. We keep on changing things in our lives in the pursuit of something better. We move from one house to another, one relationship to the next, but still we are carrying our same emotions, and we are restless.

When we have developed unshakeable faith, we naturally want to cultivate more and more wholesome actions. Whether it is wholesome thoughts, wholesome speech, or wholesome deeds, we want to focus on these positive efforts. We especially want to cultivate those good qualities which have not yet arisen in us.

As we begin to feel the benefits of wholesome activities, our enthusiasm increases. The more positive our efforts become, the more we break the old negative habitual patterns. These positive efforts will prevent future unwholesome actions from arising.

If we look honestly into our minds, into our thoughts, our speech, and our physical actions, we see how conflicted we really are! Maybe sometimes we tell lies even though we want to be honest. For whatever reason, there is a habitual pattern to tell lies that we fall into. If we look closely at our relationships, we also see that it is very possible to love and then hate the very same person or object. Love and hate go together. Why is this conflict there?

Since the day we were conceived, and throughout our entire lives, we will experience these dualistic feelings of pain and pleasure, love and hate, attachment and aversion. That's why we are never at peace.

Although all we truly want is peace, we remain very restless because we are always moving between extremes. We are never in the center. That's why faith is one of the most important energies we need in order to cultivate Right Effort.

Through our spiritual practice, our blind faith has to become clear faith. Our clear faith can then become unshakeable faith. And ultimately we have to develop faith based on wisdom. When faith is based on wisdom, it is incredibly powerful.

In the Sutras, Buddha taught that as long as we are here in samsara, so conflicted with attachment and aversion, then to us the universe will not seem perfect.

If we are always looking for perfection outside ourselves, we will not find it. Although faith cannot find perfection, it can help us to connect to the positive side of any one object. That's why some masters say that, "Faith is like a magnet which will attract all the positive things."

As we develop more and more faith, faith has the power to transform our minds. For this reason faith is one of those mental factors that has the most power to cultivate Right Effort.

Four Practices of Right Effort

Traditionally we are taught that there are four different practices related to Right Effort. First we develop faith, and we try to abandon all our negative habitual patterns at the mental level, verbal level, and at the physical level. This is the reason why the preliminary Buddhist practices emphasize accumulating so many repetitions of mantras. We have to repeat our practices over and over again in order to break unwholesome habitual patterns.

The second aspect of Right Effort is about strengthening ourselves to prevent future unwholesome actions from arising. After abandoning unwholesome patterns in our mental continuums, we then have more power to avoid future negative actions.

The third aspect of Right Effort is about increasing any positive actions we are performing at the mental, verbal, and physical levels. We try to cultivate these positive activities until we achieve some perfection.

The fourth aspect of Right Effort is about locating the positive qualities that are not yet being cultivated and then putting an effort into nurturing those qualities as well.

So these are the four practices emphasized under Right Effort. As we have discussed, Right Effort is important because it integrates all the other branches of the Noble Eightfold Path.

The Noble Eightfold Path can be divided into three categories: the training of wisdom, the training of discipline, and the training of meditation.

Right View and Right Intention are part of the training of wisdom. As we have established, wrong view is ignorance. So to counteract that ignorance we need the training of wisdom. Right View is an antidote to ignorance, which is the most fundamental destructive emotion we have.

Right Speech, Right Action, Right Livelihood and Right Effort are all part of the training of discipline, which is about disciplining the mind, disciplining the speech, and disciplining the physical actions. Discipline is when we make a resolution not to commit negative actions with our body, speech, and mind.

There are many discussions about the human tendency to engage in negative activities and about how to develop ways to stop such tendencies. The training of discipline is about refraining from those activities. Discipline is an antidote to the destructive emotion of desire.

Right Mindfulness, and Right Concentration, which we will discuss in the following chapters, are considered part of the training of meditation and are antidotes to the third destructive emotion of anger.

Q & A

Q: Lama, the basic ingredients for the practice of Guru Yoga involve pure view and faith. I was wondering if Guru Yoga could help aid the development of what we were just discussing since that ingredient of faith is ultimately so crucial?

A: Yes. Guru Yoga and sadhana meditation methods are to develop our pure vision. As a Vajrayana practitioner, as a tantric practitioner, we all receive empowerments. In an empowerment, we are introduced to our innate Buddha nature and to the realization that everyone else is also a Buddha. We are trained to see beyond our relative selves and to see the divine within each one of us.

Guru Yoga and many of these deity practices are about how to take whatever is introduced during an empowerment and bring that same outlook into our daily lives.

In tantric meditation we are the Buddha, and we visualize that we are in the pure realm of the Buddha. With this practice there is great transformation. This pure vision is introduced during an empowerment. Guru Yoga is only found in the tantric teachings of the Vajrayana. We cannot find Guru Yoga in the Mahayana or Hinayana traditions.

Within the Hinayana and Mahayana traditions, we are practicing from our current perspective as human beings. Then we are trying to achieve Buddhahood. But in the tantra we are receiving empowerments and being introduced to ourselves as already being Buddha. If we are the Buddha, then everyone is the Buddha. Even a cat is the Buddha.

That's a method to first see more purity within ourselves, so we then see more purity in the world. All our experiences are based on the conditions inside of us. If we have impure conditions, then we have an impure world. If we have pure conditions, then we have pure visions of the world around us. That is how the method works.

If we can maintain the pure outlook that was introduced in the empowerment — whether we are getting up, taking a shower, eating, sleeping — if we can maintain that same pure vision continuously, then that is the practice of Right Effort. That is the integration of all the noble paths.

Q: Lama, you mentioned a little bit about the idea of even the deepest, strongest love having accompanying hate packed into it. This definitely seems evident in some relationships. Could you speak a little bit more about the nature of this and also about practices to work on it? It seems so counterintuitive and yet so evident that people who love each other so much can also have this undesirable hate side.

A: When love is based on ego and self, then when ego and self are not fulfilled that love becomes hate. Even the faith we carry for a teacher, or for Buddha, or for the Dharma, is based on our egos in the beginning. So if our egos are not entertained, then even our feelings of faith can turn negative. We may hate the Buddha! We may hate the Dharma! Or we may start hating other people's Gods too. We may start believing "My God is good, your God is bad." All of this is our egos talking.

So the deciding factor is whether, in that deep relationship of love, love is actually transforming the ego. If that love is helping to create egolessness, then I think slowly the potentialities for hatred will dissolve. But if that love is not transforming us, if it is only strengthening our selves and egos, then our potential for hatred will also be strengthened simultaneously.

Even with meditation, first we fall into the same kind of ego-based love with our practice. But then that ego is slowly seeing its own true nature, and gradually, when the ego becomes egoless, then there will be no hatred.

Q: I'm not sure what you mean by "being good."

A: In this context "being good" means being wholesome or virtuous. Virtue and non-virtue are right and wrong. Whatever actions we do with destructive emotions are non-virtuous. And whatever mental, verbal, or physical actions we do based on positive emotions like compassion or faith, those are virtuous actions.

It all depends on whether the emotions are destructive or positive. If they are destructive, then they have more potential to bring pain to us and to others. If we kill someone with strong anger, that anger can harm us and will inflict great pain on the victim. So killing is non-virtue. But if we use love to protect someone from killing or being killed, then that's virtue. Or helping someone, that's virtue. That is a wholesome activity.

Q: How can you know the whole consequence of an action? For example, say you help someone, but in the long term it doesn't really help that person, and we hurt them inadvertently?

A: That's a good question. Helping others is very difficult. If we are at the stage of the Buddha, and we have perfect compassion and perfect wisdom, we understand our own intentions, and we know everything about the person we are trying to help, then we can act with confidence.

If we don't have such compassion based on wisdom, even compassion can be a blind emotion. We may think that we are helping someone, but at some point we discover that actually we are harming them. That's why Buddhist training emphasizes the development of wisdom and compassion first. Once we develop these qualities, then we can help others much more properly. That's why first we have to work on ourselves.

Now I'm not saying we should not try to help. We need to first examine our motivation though. If we are really helping with genuine compassion and without any expectation, then that is good. As far as we are concerned, we are sincerely, honestly, doing something to try to help them.

It's possible that sometimes it may help them, and sometimes it may harm them, but what is important is that we have a good intention. As far as whether that will translate into helping them or not, or maybe into making them become more needy, who knows?

Most of the time, until we are fully enlightened with complete compassion based on wisdom, we are not sure whether we are really helping them or not. But if we are sincere, if we have compassion, then that gives us positive karma because of such actions.

Q: Can intuition be a right path? Sometimes when we have a gut feeling about something, and we decide it is the right thing to do, we might still later realize that it was wrong.

A: At our level, when you say "intuition is right or wrong," how do you define right or wrong? Is right or wrong something based on natural karma, on virtue and non-virtue as we have been discussing, or is right and wrong based on your feelings about what may or may not be good for you? How do you define what is right or wrong, according to your intuition?

Q: Sometimes it's like an instinct.

A: Yes. So when you realize that the instinct is right or wrong, do you make that judgement based on the natural law of karma? Or do you make that judgement based on your own feelings?

If your instinct, whether it is right or wrong, is based on the natural law of karma, then I think maybe your instinct is a little bit evolved. If your instinct is against the natural law of karma, then how can you define the results as virtuous or as part of a spiritual cultivation?

Most instincts or intuitions are a by-product of habitual patterns and activities in our mental continuum. So according to those patterns, we have instincts, and we have intuitions. Intuition cannot be by chance; it has some causes and conditions.

Q: Are instinct and intuition different?

A: Maybe we can explore that question more. What is intuition? What is instinct? Are instinct and intuition just gut feelings? Are they only feelings or are they something more? So what do you think?

Q: I don't know.

A: I think they may be interchangeable in the context of your main question. But if we study the Abhidharma Kosha, then within Buddhist psychology we will have never encountered anything called "instinct." For that matter, I haven't even found anything called "intuition" in those forty-six categories of the Abhidharma Kosha, which is the most detailed psychological study in Buddhism.

But on the other hand, I think that in our daily lives we often use intuition or instinct. But the very high level meditators, the great masters, eventually have the power to go beyond time. Sometimes they can see the future in the present. They can also remember the distant past. So those are called realizations. Some yogis refer to those experiences as intuition. They see something of the future in the present, or they can remember past lifetimes in the present. But again this is only when we have very high levels of meditation, in which the mind becomes so evolved that the mind actually has some qualities of wisdom.

So sometimes those realizations have been used, but I don't think that is the same as intuition. If intuition is based on the natural law of karma, then this is a way to determine what is right and wrong.

But if intuition is based on our feelings, then most of the time we will define right and wrong according to our egos, and this has less to do with the natural law of karma.

Chapter Nine
The Noble Eightfold Path - Right Mindfulness

The seventh branch of the Noble Eightfold path is Right Mindfulness. Right Mindfulness is divided into the Four Foundations of Mindfulness. These Four Foundations are: mindfulness of the body, mindfulness of feeling, mindfulness of mental consciousness, and mindfulness of mental phenomena. To understand Right Mindfulness, we need to understand the nature of all conditioned things. The Buddha categorized conditioned things into the five aggregates: form, feeling, ideation, formation, and consciousness.

Mindfulness of the Body

The first foundation of mindfulness is mindfulness of the body. Mindfulness of the body corresponds with the first aggregate of form or matter. All material things are composed of elemental atoms of earth, water, fire, and air. Whatever is created from these atoms is called "matter." Our physical bodies are also composed of these elements. We interact with the world around us through our six sense organs.

These are called sense organs because through them we can perceive the entire material world. Because we have an eye organ, we can see visual objects. Whatever we see is matter. Because we have an ear organ we can hear sounds. Sound is also matter. Everything we can smell and taste and touch with our bodies is matter. The sixth sense organ of the mind and mental consciousness also perceives phenomena in the material world.

There are many ways to study matter. Biologists and chemists examine the components of matter. Physicists study matter and it's motion through space and time. The Buddhist way of studying matter is to intellectually study its properties and then to use meditation to overcome all of the emotions related with matter.

Whatever sensory objects we experience, through our sense organs and through our minds, become the causes and conditions for different emotions to arise. When we see something agreeable, we are attracted to it, and we get attached. When we see something repulsive, it gives us pain and suffering, and we may get angry.

Every sense organ has it's corresponding sense object. For example, the sense organ of the eye has the visual objects. The sense organ of the ear has the sense object of sound. Each sense organ, when interacting with the sense objects, has the power to elicit different emotions in us.

Buddhists don't wish to manipulate atoms for some ordinary worldly incentive, such as seeking monetary gain. The main purpose of studying the material world through Buddhism is to learn how to overcome the causes and conditions of destructive emotions.

There are some schools of Buddhism, like the materialists, the realist philosophers, who conduct a rigorous study of phenomena. But their main purpose is to overcome all of the afflictive emotions. For this reason they practice meditation.

When we speak of this aspect of mindfulness called "mindfulness of the body," we include not only our own physical bodies but also all other physical bodies and the material world.

Intellectual study of phenomena cannot free us from destructive emotions. To overcome all the emotions, we have to look deeper and deeper through meditation. Mindfulness gives us insight into the material components of our bodies as well as into the outside material world. But this insight also extends well beyond the scope of what is apparent.

Apparent things are objects perceived through our first five sense organs. But the insight we gain through mindfulness is more profound and has more to do with the sixth sense organ of mental consciousness.

Insight is gained through a meditative state of mind. In Buddhism this is considered a sixth sense organ, which is known as the mind or mental consciousness. When that mind is sharpened through meditation, and our insight grows deeper and deeper, we may see something which we have never seen before.

Ordinarily our perceptions remain at a very gross level. Through mindfulness though, we are able to see something which is far more subtle. With this meditative insight, all material objects are recognized as part of mindfulness of body. As our insight becomes more refined, we see a greater truth or reality. Reality will appear very different from how we had previously seen the phenomenal world.

There is a big difference between how we see a material object, and how the Noble Ones, the enlightened masters, see the same object. I think the enlightened ones see the purity in all things. They have reached the third level of seeing, which is the level of pure vision.

Without that pure vision, what we see in the world is based on our karma. How we perceive the outer world is actually entirely based on our inner conditions. For example, when we see something visually alluring, some color or shape we are attracted to, that beauty is not necessarily inherent to that object. As the saying goes, "Beauty lies in the eye of the beholder."

In Buddhist understanding, attraction and aversion are a result of our emotions and karma. This karma is based on our past habitual patterns. When something generates an agreeable condition within us, when we feel very drawn to something, it is considered a "karmic link." Based on our past experiences, we have developed an affinity for certain objects or places or people.

All of these experiences of outer objects are based on what yogis call the "karmic vision." These perceptions are all based on our individual karma. That's why what we experience is not a universal truth.

For example, while humans can see a certain color or shape, cats and dogs may have a very different relationship to these same visual objects. And even among humans, our perception of each object, and our resulting emotions, are as individual as our respective karmas.

How we perceive reality, at our level, is based entirely on our inner conditions. That's why it's called "karmic vision." Karmic visions are personal as well as collective. When we speak of "collective karma," it refers to the fact that certain groups of beings perceive things in a similar way. For example, humans have certain shared visions of reality. But within humanity, each person still has his or her own personal karma which is unique.

As humans, we experience some things in an agreeable way. Within such collectively agreeable experiences, we can still have personally disagreeable responses. This has more to do with our karma than with the object itself.

This is why Buddha said that these personal karmic experiences are all relative. These experiences are not independent or universal. We often try to project a collective karmic experience as being universally true. When we conduct a thorough investigation, however, it becomes clear that this is not the case.

We have to start from where we are though. All the great Buddhist philosophers agree that we have to use the relative truth in order to see the ultimate truth.

Through meditative experience, we have to go deeper and deeper into our exploration of the nature of reality. Are all our material experiences now only relative truths? If so, then what is the ultimate truth? These are the questions that yogis are trying to answer through meditation.

This mindfulness of the body includes mindfulness of all material things. As long as we are in the desire realm or in the form realm, we will remain in a physical body. We have to use our personal experiences of our own physical bodies to understand outer phenomena. Since all material objects are composed of these same elemental atoms, we can know outer objects through mindfulness of our own bodies.

The only difference between us and the outer inanimate objects, is that we are psychosomatic beings, operating from this interaction of mind and body. It is only consciousness that separates all sentient beings from other physical matter.

As sentient beings, we are capable of awareness which leads us to exploration. But the mind and body also create great obstacles. When we possess all these emotions and karmic propensities, everything becomes a very complex puzzle.

In order to better understand this, Buddha taught about the five aggregates, the twelve ayatanas (bases), and the eighteen dhatus (elements). He taught these aspects in order for us to look deeper and deeper into the nature of things. Mindfulness of the body allows us to examine the nature of the material world.

Mindfulness of Feelings

The second foundation of mindfulness is mindfulness of feelings, which corresponds with the second aggregate of feeling. Feelings are experienced through the mind and body. Buddha taught that there are five different kinds of feelings. There are physical feelings of pain and pleasure, mental feelings of happiness and unhappiness, and neutral feelings. Neutral feelings can be physical, mental, or both.

Feeling is one of the most important aspects of our lives and personalities. Feeling plays such a big role in our experience because it is based directly on our egos and on our sense of self. Most of the things we do in our lives are motivated by our wish to feel more pleasure and happiness and to avoid pain and suffering. Most of the major decisions we make in our lives are based on our feelings rather than our intellects.

When we practice mindfulness of feelings, we examine where a sensation and/or a feeling is coming from. Through meditative insight we question the nature and properties of that feeling. Mindfulness of feeling allows us to know the basis of a particular reaction.

We treasure and cherish feelings of pleasure and happiness. As a result we get very attached to these rewarding experiences. This drives us to try harder and harder to attain more of these positive feelings.

Feeling is crucial to our human experience. As a result of our attachment to ourselves, we are easily subject to having hurt feelings. The minute someone says or does something that threatens our egos, we respond with pain or sadness or anger.

Everything we do in our lives is based on our desire for happiness and pleasure. The whole entertainment industry is built on our wish to feel good and on our need to be distracted from ourselves and our uncomfortable feelings. We find pleasure in watching movies about other people's emotional dramas. It allows us to forget ourselves and to feel less alone in our human experience.

Through meditative insight, we can come to see the true nature of our feelings. We can understand the source of these feelings and the ways in which they impact our reality. This is the second foundation — mindfulness of feeling.

Mindfulness of the Mind

The third foundation of mindfulness is mindfulness of mind and mental consciousness. This corresponds with the fifth aggregate Buddha taught, which is the aggregate of consciousness.

Consciousness arises in the mind. Each of the six sense organs have corresponding sense objects, which we have described. For example, the sense organ of the eye has the sense object of visual objects etc.

Each of these six sense objects also has a corresponding sense consciousness. When we see, when we hear, when we taste, when we experience any of the six sense objects, basic consciousness arises in the mind.

Take, for example, the eyes; when we see a visual object, then mind arises as eye consciousness. Eye consciousness is the part of the mind that becomes present when a healthy eye organ and a visual object come together.

It takes all three of these factors — the eye organ, the visual object and the eye consciousness — for visual perception to arise in the present moment. If one of these three factors is missing, then we will not be able to see.

Buddha taught that these six consciousnesses are present. But just because they are present doesn't mean that they are not still based on emotions and defilements. Although we perceive these apparent objects with our present consciousness, our projections are still based on the inner conditions of the basic mind. This basic mind is always traveling with us from moment to moment, from life to life, filled with emotions and karma which then determine how these sense organs experience the world around us.

This foundation of mindfulness of the mind or mental consciousness, is to see the true nature of these six sense consciousnesses. Where do they come from? Are they present all the time? What are their properties? Through meditation we will begin to see the nature of consciousness more clearly.

Mindfulness of Dharma or Phenomena

The fourth foundation of mindfulness is called the foundation of dharma. Here dharma does not have the usual meaning of Buddhist teachings. In this context dharma means all phenomena. This fourth foundation corresponds with the aggregates of ideation and formation. That fourth aggregate of formation is very complex and includes the entire Buddhist understanding of psychology. This is outlined thoroughly in the texts of the Abhidharma.

The aggregates of ideation and formation are included in the fourth foundation, which is mindfulness of dharma or mental phenomena. As long as we have all these thoughts inside our minds, we create karma. Karma is the origin of all our experiences in our lives. As we have discussed, our entire experience of reality is based on our individual and collective karmic vision.

As long as we have karmic vision, then nothing is universal. Dharma does not include those first three foundations, our physical bodies, our feelings or sensations, and our sense consciousnesses. But everything else we experience is included in this fourth foundation of mindfulness of dharma. Here we find insight into Buddhist psychology and into all the different kinds of mental actions.

When I say "psychology," I am referring to all the root positive and negative emotions and to all our mental activities. We usually say that desire, anger, and ignorance are the three fundamental destructive emotions. However, this fourth foundation of mindfulness of the dharma includes all the destructive emotions, as well as all the positive emotions like faith, concentration, and memory. It also includes all the neutral emotions. We have many mental activities.

Our minds are constantly filled with these mental activities. Our mental actions respond to what occurs circumstantially, to our interactions with an apparent object. At any given moment, anger, or jealousy, or attachment might take over the mind, based on some internal or external event.

Whenever the mind interacts with an object, through the sense organs or through mental projections, a strong emotion is activated. Although we may feel that the whole mind is suddenly experiencing anger, we must remember that the sleeping emotions are still existing in us. We may think that when we have strong anger we do not have any love. But love is still there inside us as a sleeping emotion. We tend to only focus on the emotions that are actively present.

All of the conflicting emotions are existing in our minds, but whenever one emotion overtakes all the others, we forget the sleeping emotions. We also forget the true nature of the mind.

This is the reason why the higher tantric teachings reveal that all the destructive emotions, by nature, are actually wisdom. In tantra we have all these wrathful deities, and we say they are arising out of wisdom. This profound practice is based on an understanding of this basic composition of our minds.

This fourth foundation of mindfulness of dharma is the most complex and includes more of the aggregates. The first foundation of mindfulness relates simply to matter. The second foundation of mindfulness refers only to feeling or sensation. The third foundation of mindfulness is related solely to the fifth aggregate of consciousness. But this fourth foundation of mindfulness includes the aggregates of ideations and formations. This fourth foundation includes all of a person's mental activities, emotions, and psychology.

Insight of Impermanence

When we investigate our experience through these Four Foundations of Mindfulness, we see the nature of outside objects as well as the nature of our internal projection of objects. We attempt to understand this in order to overcome the ego and to gain a more noble understanding.

The more we examine these four foundations of mindfulness, the more we realize that they are all impermanent. Our physical bodies and matter are impermanent. Our feelings, our consciousness, and all of the core emotions are impermanent. They are changing every moment.

When we see something beautiful, or when we feel something pleasurable, it brings us happiness, and we get attached to those objects or that experience. When we grow attached to an object or an experience, we try to make it permanent. This creates so much conflict and unhappiness because it is impossible to make that experience last.

Only through meditation will we learn to see the true nature of things. The more we meditate, the more we will see that every moment our physical bodies are changing. Every moment our feelings are changing. Every moment our minds are changing. Every moment our emotions are changing. So we come to accept impermanence.

Impermanence is the opposite of our wishes and our desires. We all want to have a permanently healthy body. So when our bodies begin to age and to decay, they become a great source of mental and physical pain.

This pain is not only a result of these changes in our bodies, but this suffering is based largely on our egos. Our egos believe that our bodies should be young and beautiful forever. Our egos strongly resist the conditioned nature of things.

We believe that having these wonderful young bodies and all these fresh material things will bring us more pleasure. But the truth is that even when these things bring us happiness in our youth, they are sowing seeds of future suffering. Inevitably we will lose these strong agile bodies and these wonderful possessions, and that loss will bring us pain.

Insight into Suffering

As long as we have feelings, they are based on ego. And as long as anything is based on ego, it is based on the root destructive emotions. Due to this fact, then even pleasure and happiness are also part of the destructive emotions.

Eventually we will come to see that all feelings and pleasures based on our bodies and sensations, or based on ideas and emotions, are actually a form of suffering.

The more deeply we look, the more we will recognize the reality of the Second Noble Truth, the origin of suffering. Whatever is impermanent and changing and aging is creating suffering.

The origin of suffering is very hard to accept because it goes against the wishes of our egos. Our egos are wishing for pleasure and happiness all the time. Our natural condition of suffering is the opposite of how we want to feel.

If we return to our early discussion of the First Noble Truth of suffering, we see that Buddha taught that suffering includes all feelings, even pleasurable and neutral feelings. This is because all feelings are based on the destructive emotions of the ego.

Buddha didn't teach the Noble Truth of suffering and mindfulness of suffering in order to make us more miserable! Students sometimes ask me, "We already have so much pain and suffering in our lives, why does Buddha have to tell us that even our pleasure is suffering?" The reason that Buddha taught this was to help us achieve complete freedom from suffering. In order to achieve this we have to be realistic and pragmatic. Insight related with suffering is critical to understanding the path to freedom.

Insight of Insubstantiality

When we delve deeper, breaking down matter to the atomic level, or examining the causes of emotions, we come to see that everything is insubstantial. We cannot find any permanence. There is no inherent existence of even a subatomic particle.

Even physicists and psychologists are reaching the same conclusions. The more they investigate, the more they agree that there is no permanent basis for matter, feelings, ideas, and all phenomena.

Insight of Emptiness

The fourth insight is that not only are these things insubstantial, but their very nature is emptiness. Matter is empty. Feeling is empty. Mind is empty. All of the emotions are empty. Those who are enlightened and who have achieved nirvāṇa realize this empty nature through the mindfulness of these Four Foundations. That is how they achieve enlightenment. Then they are finally free from all pain and suffering.

The more we investigate, the more there is to see. From impermanence we see emptiness. From emptiness we see the ultimate truth or ultimate nature. This realization is the purpose of The Four

Foundations of Mindfulness, which are taught primarily in the Theravadan or Hinayana Buddhist tradition. This is the main practice within countries such as Burma, Thailand, and Sri Lanka.

In the Mahayana tradition, in texts like The Heart Sutra, we also learn that, "Form is emptiness, emptiness is form; form is no other than emptiness, emptiness is no other than form." In the Vajrayana Buddhist tradition we have very profound sadhana meditation practices, which provide the deepest insight into this emptiness nature.

All these traditions are complimentary. The purpose of The Four Foundations of Mindfulness is to reveal the emptiness nature of all of our five aggregates. When we see that the natures of form, feeling, ideation, formation, and consciousness are all emptiness, then we have the realization of selflessness.

Here, for the first time, we see the true face of our egos, which is egolessness. We see the true nature of the self, which is selflessness. At this point we begin to free ourselves from ignorance.

When we're free from ignorance, we're free from attachment and aversion. At that point we no longer create any karma. We experience the whole universe, including our personal experiences, as pure vision.

As long as we have egos, we will continue to have karmic experiences. Right Mindfulness is based on The Four Foundations of Mindfulness, which will ultimately lead us to pure vision and to the ultimate truth of selflessness. This is the purpose of all insight meditation.

Q & A

Q: When applying The Four Foundations of Mindfulness in my meditation I can more easily see interdependence, impermanence, and the true causes of suffering. Then I go out of meditation, and see, for instance, a nice car. Immediately I think it's independent, permanent, and therefore the cause of happiness. My question is how to keep the understanding I gained from the cushion and apply such an understanding in my daily life?

A: I think that through more and more meditation we can transform our minds. Through such transformation we can integrate this understanding into every aspect of our lives. Then we will come to accept change and the nature of reality without reacting. At that point we can become more and more like witnesses.

When we practice meditation, there will be a change inside of us, and we will develop more equanimity. After leaving our meditation cushions, we may still have reactions such as you described.

If our meditation is not good, then when our meditation is done, we will revert to those habitual patterns. On the other hand, if our meditation is gradually improving, then some transformations will likely occur that will extend beyond our meditation session.

The meditations we do are for the purpose of changing our habitual patterns and emotions. When such a change occurs, it will have a lasting effect. Maybe then, when we see that attractive car, we will realize that one day everything will get old, and we will not even be able to drive! One day we will have to leave everything behind, including our own bodies! This understanding will help put our attachments to worldly possessions into perspective.

Attachment is the strongest of the afflictive emotions here in the desire realm. The best antidote for desire is contemplating impermanence and death. The more we practice meditation on impermanence, and the more we meditate on death, the more we realize that at the time of death we cannot take our physical bodies with us.

At the time of death we will see the futility in so many of the worldly things we have accumulated. No matter how many billions of dollars we have, money will not be able to save us from our own deaths.

Throughout history, we have seen many strange reactions to death. In Asia there were some kings or lords who had very strong attachment to their lives and belongings. When they were dying they ordered that all their horses, and even their own family members, be killed and buried alongside of them amidst all their possessions.

I have heard that even here in America some people freeze their bodies, hoping that at some point scientists will find some cure for death.

Although none of us want to die, it's going to happen. When the eye is gone, how will we perceive beauty? That's what we have to remember when we are attracted to beautiful objects. One day even our eyes will be gone.

Much of the time we keep ourselves busy and live in denial. But this denial is not going to stop us from experiencing impermanence. Even while we are in denial, the clock is ticking. We may be rushing around busily in our lives, doing so many things, but still we are moving towards our own deaths .

This is the reason why that first insight of impermanence is so powerful. It brings us a new understanding of the truth. The death of someone we love creates a deep awareness of impermanence. And when we meditate on our own deaths, everything becomes very different.

But many of us are in denial; that's how we live life. We expect to somehow be exempt from old age and death. We ignore the truth. Through the insights realized by the great yogis and meditators, we can begin to transform ourselves and accept the truth of our lives.

No one wants to die. That's why death generally involves so much suffering. Although all feelings are suffering, we still get attached to feelings of pleasure and happiness. Although everything is insubstantial, we are still attached to the idea of substantiality. Our minds create and reinforce these conditions.

Although the truth is that everything is empty, we ignore that truth and remain deeply attached to a self and an ego. What we perceive as real is often the opposite of the truth. This is why we have so much suffering. So doing more meditation on impermanence and death is the best antidote for those feelings.

Q: When we practice meditation do we experience mindfulness in the order we studied it - first there's matter, and then feelings, then consciousness, and then dharma - or can it come differently depending on our karma and our personal patterns?

A: Mindfulness is considered the seventh branch of the Noble Eightfold Path, and concentration, which we will discuss next, is the eighth branch. When we meditate, we first have to do the path of concentration. We have to start with shamatha meditation, and when our concentration and attention are good, then we can do the mindfulness practices of insight meditation or vipassana. In our own meditation within the mindfulness practices, we don't necessarily have to go in that same order of the Four Foundations. Really the type of mindfulness we will apply in our insight meditation will depend on what we are thinking about. Whatever is distracting us — whether it's our bodies, our feelings, our ideas — will be where we need to apply that mindfulness. This could happen in any order, depending on our emotional involvements, our attachments, and our feelings.

Whatever strong emotions we have, these objects and emotions will arise in our meditation sessions to distract us from the objects of meditation. So it could be a different order, depending on the person.

The Four Foundations of Mindfulness are presented in this particular order because they go from the gross to the subtle. Matter is the most gross. Matter is something tangible that we experience. Next comes our feelings, our minds, and finally the most subtle mindfulness of mental phenomena. But what will arise for us personally in our meditation, depends on our habitual patterns and emotions. According to these, we may have different experiences.

Q: What is an example of a neutral emotion?

A: A neutral emotion is one which is neither positive nor negative. So it is neutral like memory. Memory can be neutral. Attention can be neutral. Although a neutral emotion can work with both positive and negative emotions, by nature a neutral emotion is neither positive nor destructive. A destructive emotion is an emotion like anger. Anger is destructive because it can bring more pain and suffering to ourselves and to others. Love is positive.

Q: Lama, do you consider emotions and feelings to be the same, or different, or both?

A: Feeling is part of emotion, but feeling is not the only aspect of emotion. When I say emotion, I refer to many aspects. Usage of the word "emotion" has changed over time.

Sometimes "emotion" refers only to a physically apparent emotion, like when we are happy and smiling. "Emotions" in that case refer to how we physically express a feeling. But in this teaching today I'm using the term "emotion" as defined within Buddhist psychology, where emotion refers to all kinds of mental activities.

Feeling is one of those mental activities. Anger is also emotion, and anger is a mental activity. Ignorance is a mental activity. Attachment is "emotion," as is jealousy.

In the Abhidharma Kosha, there are forty-six mental activities. In the Abhidharma Samuccaya text there are fifty-one mental activities defined. The word "emotion" refers to all of those mental activities. Those are all emotions and activities, and feeling is just one of those activities.

Q: So "emotion" would be the umbrella?

A: Yes, the umbrella for all mental activities. If we look in a dictionary, we may find "emotion" defined according to our time period and culture. In Tibetan though we call emotion "sems byung." In Sanskrit it's call "chaitta," which means mind and mental activities. All those mental activities are "emotions." I am referring to all those mental activities. Feeling is just one of them.

Q: You had mentioned about sense consciousness, and that in order to see, there are three factors that must come together. What are those three factors?

A: In order to see something visually, like when I see you, I need you as an object. Then I also need a physically healthy eye organ. I also need eye consciousness to see you. Only when these three factors come together can we have the experience of seeing.

When one factor is missing, then we will be blind. To see, we need these three interdependencies: object, eye organ, and eye consciousness. Even if I have a healthy eye organ, but my mind is distracted somewhere else, I may not see you. Or if my mind is present, but my eye organ is blind, then I also cannot see you, even though I am paying attention.

Even if consciousness is arising and the eye is healthy but you are very far away from me, then I cannot see you. So the object also has to be present in order for our eye to see it.

These three factors have to come together for a person to have the experience of seeing. According to Buddhist psychology, this consciousness is present when all three factors come together.

Later I may mentally recall what I have captured with my eyes. It will reappear in my mind as a memory. There is no eye consciousness in that memory, however, because the object and the eye organ are no longer involved in that experience. I am remembering what I have seen, so there's no eye consciousness.

As we have discussed, there are six sense consciousnesses corresponding to the six sense organs. That sixth organ is the mind and mental consciousness. It is mind consciousness we use when we practice shamatha meditation. Through such practice we are trying to connect to our basic mind, to our present mind.

Q: When you recall something, it is in your memory. Your eyes are closed, you don't have the organ, you don't have the object, but you're still seeing something visual in your mind. Wouldn't that still be considered "eye consciousness?"

A: I don't think so. That is only memory in the basic mind.

Q: So you don't need those three factors of sense organ, sense object, and sense consciousness in memory?

A: No. You are just remembering what you have seen in the past.

Q: But where does it come from? What is generating those pictures?

A: Visual memory is the experience of seeing something that has been impressed into our basic minds. Then because of the strength of that impression, when we remember, such a memory generates those images.

We are conceived with this basic mind, and it will continue even after death. That is the basis for rebirth. After death, we don't have eyes; we don't have ears. Our bodies are cremated, and all the organs are gone from us, but still there is a basic mind that is continuing. That basic mind is where all our emotions, according to our habitual patterns, are impressed, all our volitions are impressed. That mind carries all our impressions and habitual patterns.

So this is how memory functions. Based on our habitual patterns, we remember things. It's the same mind when we go to sleep at night, and the same mind in the morning when we get up. It is the same mind that remembers to make coffee because it had coffee yesterday. That basic mind continues even in the afterlife, along with those habitual tendencies.

Q: But when you are reincarnated, those impressions seem to disappear.

A: Yes and no. This depends on our experience. Death is similar to a good sleep. When we have a very deep sleep, do we remember anything that we have done yesterday or in the past? When we get up in the morning, do we recall any past experiences?

Q: Of course.

A: Death is similar to sleep. Death is just the separation of our physical bodies from our basic minds. But according to our experiences, whatever strong emotions we are attached to, we will remember such emotions even after death.

Death is only the moment where mind and body are separated.

After that, basic mind still continues. In the mind we carry all our memories, based on our past experiences. The memories that will stay with us depend on the strength of our attachments, our aversions, and our emotional involvements with those objects and experiences.

The more we are attached to something, the more we will remember it. The more we are angry with someone, the more that enemy will come into our memory or into our dreams. So sleep is like a small death, but the mind is continuing.

Q: Lama, When you talk about basic mind and main mind, are they the same kun gzhi nam shes?

A: Yes, we can say that. "Kun gzhi" is usually a term given by the "mind only" school of Buddhism. Some other schools use that term as well to describe the basic mind. What we are referring to is the mind that is continuing after death.

Q: When I meditate, what is more important: observing my thoughts and what's going on inside of me and inside of my mind, or focusing on experiencing the present moment by focusing on the breath? Are these two different types of meditation?

A: When you say "observing," how do you observe in meditation?

Q: Thoughts arise. They come and then they go.

A: So do you go after the thoughts when you observe them?

Q: No, it depends. Sometimes I realize I have a thought. Then I kind of let it go. It comes and goes.

A: At that point where your mind is observing, is there an object or not? Thought is coming and going, so when you don't follow the thought, where is your mind?

Q: I don't know

 A: Nowhere?

Q: I mean, I see the thought, and I understand, "Oh I have this thought." And then I'm like, "oh, ok."

A: There is insight meditation where we focus on mindfulness. And there is shamatha meditation where we focus on one object, like our breath or a blue flower.

The mind is a complex thing. Within the mind we can have both a subject and an object. There's a thought and there's a thinker. So who is the meditator? Without a thinker we cannot have thought.

But if we are still thinking thoughts, then I don't think that's meditation. Meditation is within the mind. Within the mind there are many emotions. Meditation is cultivating attention. Attention is usually cultivated by not forgetting an object. That's why we use breathing. When we use breathing as the object of shamatha meditation, then the mind is trying to focus attention on the breath, and every moment we are remembering the object of meditation.

When we forget that object, and the mind is remembering something else, then we are distracted. See? So that distraction is not meditation.

Meditation is directed attention. We need to counteract a mind which is always distracted. Early in our meditation practice we have to constantly redirect our attention back to the object because our minds are going somewhere else.

We try to bring the mind back to the object of meditation. We try to remain in that state where we remember that object in every single moment.

By doing that, we are cultivating attention within the mind. Attention is a neutral emotion. We are trying to see how long we can pay attention. The more we think, the less attention we have.

In the beginning of meditation we will witness how difficult it is to pay attention to one object. To extend that attention longer and longer, we are trying to free ourselves from excitement and distraction due to too much thought. If we keep forgetting the object, it's like a form of Attention Deficit Disorder.

The more attention we have, the longer we will focus continually on the breath. Meditation is to extend our attention. Out of that attention, we will then have more mindfulness to see the nature of that object.

So once we have good attention, then we will have more mindfulness. Then with mindfulness, at some point we will have both attention and mindfulness together. They are developed upon each other. We cannot have mindfulness without attention. They come together at some point.

Q: So at some point you experience attention on an object and what's going on around you at the same time?

A: Exactly! That's the whole purpose. Then, in that attention, we can have insight and obtain wisdom. This is how to see wisdom by using attention and mindfulness. At that point there's no thinker, and there's no thought.

Chapter Ten

The Noble Eightfold Path - Right Concentration

The final branch of the Noble Eightfold Path is "Right Concentration." As we know, the main obstacle to good meditation is distraction. The more distracting our lives become, the more difficult it is to focus our attention. So not only are we missing these important elements of attention and concentration, but distraction also brings more negativities into our lives.

If we investigate the sources of these constant distractions, we will see that they are all rooted in the destructive emotions. The more ignorance we have, the more anger and attachment we have in our mental streams, the less attention we will have.

This constant state of distractibility produces more negative karma. Without attention, we are much less aware of our physical actions, our speech, and our thoughts. When we act without true awareness, we are creating causes and conditions for future suffering.

At a worldly level, this constant mental distraction also prevents us from performing well at our jobs. It interferes with our ability to communicate well with the people around us and to achieve success because we simply cannot focus our attention on the task in front of us. Instead we are always daydreaming. We are thinking about the past or the future. We are wondering what we'll eat for lunch, or wishing we were doing something else. Often we are obsessing about something someone said that hurt our feelings.

Mental distraction impacts all facets of our lives. If you are a student, and your mind is constantly wandering, it can be extremely challenging to study properly or to write a term paper. If you are working at a stressful job, then your inability to concentrate on the task at hand can impact your performance. If you are in a relationship, and you cannot be present to your children or to your partner because you are always thinking about other things, then you will experience conflict and disappointment within your family.

If we look closely in this way, we see that distraction is not just an issue when it comes time to meditate. Distraction is actually impacting our lives on every level, and meditation is the first step in beginning to examine those habitual patterns.

If we do not begin to break down those habitual patterns through meditation while we are alive, then even when we die that distracted mind will continue. After death, we will experience the bardo stage as a series of rushing distracted dreams, and we will take rebirth with that same disoriented mind.

When the mind is plagued with distractions, it is said to resemble a waterfall. All the emotions and all the karma come rushing over us, pushing us further and further down, producing more and more negativities.

The main cause of distraction is our unexamined destructive emotions. This is especially true for us humans living here in the desire realm. This realm is filled with craving and attachment. We are driven by our need for desirable objects to consume.

Out of all of these objects of attachment, our strongest desire is for other humans. Our other greatest attachment is towards the objects which we wish to possess. Our need for human relationships and our desire to have many possessions are driving forces in our lives.

The most direct method to overcome distraction is through meditation. At the highest level, we reach this state of concentration or "samadhi."

There are four different levels of concentration in the form realm and four levels in the formless realm. These eight levels are all considered worldly concentrations. These meditations in the form and formless realms can help you calm your emotions and achieve deep peace. But these worldly concentrations don't necessarily help you transcend all three realms of samsara to achieve complete liberation.

In the Theravada or Hinayana tradition of meditation, the aim of meditation practice is to achieve the nirvāṇa and to go beyond samsara entirely. The method of practice in the Theravadan tradition is based entirely on renunciation. Renunciation means seeing that the nature of our lives is pain and suffering. Due to this realization we then wish to renounce the whole cycle of suffering and to achieve the cessation, the nirvāṇa.

Shamatha Meditation

Based on this renunciation, we then practice shamatha meditation. Shamatha is also known as "calm-abiding" meditation. According to the texts of the Abhidharma, there are two methods for practicing shamatha meditation.

The first method is to use shamatha practice as an antidote to desire. Since we live in the desire realm, desire is the strongest destructive emotion for us humans. In order to overcome this strong, active desire and attachment, we need to know why we have these emotions.

The Four Objects of Attachment

Shamatha meditation can help us to overcome the four objects of attachment. These objects are: color, shape, touch, and attention. When we examine desire more closely, we will see that our desire for visual objects is especially strong. We are drawn to objects because of their color, shape, design, and all of their appealing visual characteristics.

Our sense of touch is also a strong source of attachment. We want something to feel good to us. Whether it is the touch of another person, the feel of something soft under our hands, or even the feel of warm sunlight on our skin, touch is something we crave. Anything tangible that we find pleasurable can become a source of attachment.

The fourth object of attachment is attention. We crave the attention of others. We crave recognition and appreciation and love. We want to do well in our lives and achieve some level of success.

Shamatha meditation can help us to overcome these four objects of attachment by giving us antidotes. In order to overcome our attachment to color, we have to do shamatha practice based on undesirable color. In order to overcome our desire for shape, then we have to do shamatha meditation on an undesirable shape.

For example, if we are attached to the beautiful body of someone we desire, then we can meditate on that shape becoming very unattractive. If we are attached to the feel of something being smooth or soft, then we have to do shamatha meditation on an undesirable texture. If we are attached to recognition, then we can meditate on the negative side effects of that attention.

Shamatha Meditation on a Corpse or Skeleton

Meditation on a human corpse is a very effective method for counteracting these objects of attachment. The Abhidharma texts describe nine meditations on a corpse, to work through these four different attachments.

Buddha said that if we cannot meditate on the specific color or shape of the corpse, if that is too gruesome or challenging at first, then we can also just meditate on the skeleton. The skeleton has the antidotal power to overcome all of the four objects of attachment. So this is how, through our practice, we try to overcome the strong, active desire and attachment so that our shamatha meditation will be effective.

Shamatha Meditation on the Breath

The second method of shamatha meditation is designed for those people who have lots of concepts, lots of thoughts, lots of inner chattering all the time. This inner chatter is not necessarily related to attachment and desire. It can include anger, neutral thoughts, and all the intellectual distractions.

When the mind is very busy in this way, it is very good to do shamatha meditation focused on the breath. The Abhidharma texts describe six different ways to use the breathing as an object of meditation.

The first breathing meditation is called "counting." You can count to ten over and over again. Beginning on the inhalation you count "one," and on the exhalation you count "two." Each time you get distracted you return again to the beginning. It is emphasized that you should not count higher than ten, or it could make you more active and distracted. It is also advised that you don't count fewer than ten, or you may become lazy in your practice.

The second breathing meditation is called "following." In this exercise you have to follow the movement of the inhalation, the circulation of the air inside you, and then the exhalation. In this way, you try to follow the movement of the air in your body.

The third breathing meditation is called "placing." With "placing" you pay complete attention to the movement of the breath in your body. With concentration you focus on the circulation of the breath from the nostrils down to the feet and back up again, like a rope of air. When you concentrate in this manner, you see that the air is continuously circulating. You can notice the temperature of the air. When you can focus your concentration on the whole circulation of the air simultaneously, then that is the third shamatha practice called "placing."

The fourth practice is called "more placing." By observing the movement of the air inside you, you begin to have the realization that air is not just composed of the air element. As your shamatha practice strengthens, you begin to experience that air contains all four elements. You also begin to realize that air is supporting the mind and the emotions. Through this you begin to see that air is actually integral to all the five aggregates. So this fourth practice of "more placing" deepens your concentration on the breath.

The fifth practice is called "modification." With modification, you use whatever concentration you have achieved based on the air meditations to increase the cultivation of spirituality inside of you.

This in turn allows you to achieve higher and higher levels of realization. The concentration is applied in order to increase the positive spiritual qualities and then decrease the negative destructive emotions.

The sixth practice is called "complete purification." You use that "modification" practice to continue cultivating the positive spiritual qualities and to completely purify all the destructive emotions and negativities. Eventually this cultivation will help you to go beyond all the negative emotions and negative karma.

We can choose the object of our shamatha meditation depending on our temperaments. If we have lots of clinging and desire, we can do shamatha meditation on the corpse or skeleton. And if we are filled with many ideas and concepts, we can quiet the mind by doing the shamatha meditation on the breath.

Both of these objects of meditation include the nine stages of shamatha. The first three stages of shamatha are to overcome the distractions, so you can pay attention to the object. The next three stages are to strengthen that attention. The last three stages of shamatha use the attention you have achieved and apply it to the result, which is concentration.

After achieving some experience with shamatha meditation, you can proceed to the next meditation which is mindfulness practice or insight meditation. Mindfulness practice is based on the seventh branch of the Noble Eightfold path. Only when you have good shamatha practice and concentration will you be able to use that attention to achieve the insight meditation.

For insight meditation, you start with the Four Foundations of Mindfulness, which we have discussed in an earlier chapter. Through cultivating Mindfulness of the Body, you have the realization that the physical body is the base of all suffering, and that helps you to accept the First Noble Truth of suffering.

As a result of our physical bodies, we are subjected to all three kinds of suffering. Because we have a physical body, we experience the suffering of suffering, and we are unable to avoid sickness and pain. Because of our physical bodies, we also have the suffering of change since nothing pleasurable can last. Furthermore, as a result of our physical bodies, we will all be subjected to old age and death, and we will have to experience the suffering of conditioned existence.

Through practicing Mindfulness of the Body, we come to recognize that this physical body is the base of all three kinds of suffering. This leads us to a profound understanding of the First Noble Truth of suffering.

The second mindfulness practice is Mindfulness of Feelings. When we look more closely, we realize that feelings are the cause of all our craving. This craving creates all the causes and conditions for our afflictive emotions and suffering. By practicing Mindfulness of Feelings, we will come to the realization that feeling is the origin of all our suffering. This will deepen our understanding of the Second Noble Truth of the origin of suffering .

The third mindfulness practice is Mindfulness of the Mind. Through this practice, we come to the realization that mind is impermanent, and mind can cease. At the present moment, our minds are the basis for the self. But through the practice of Mindfulness of the Mind, we can develop insight into the Third Noble Truth of cessation.

The fourth mindfulness practice is Mindfulness of the Dharma, which in this context means phenomena. Through this practice we come to see that within the dharma there are things to abandon, and there are things to accept. Based on learning what to accept and what to reject, we will come to know the Fourth Noble Truth of the path.

Including the Four Foundations of Mindfulness, there are thirty-seven noble practices from the Theravadan tradition that instruct us on how to achieve the nirvāṇa.

The Mahayana tradition takes this concentration to another level. After taking the Bodhisattva vow, we cultivate loving-kindness and compassion. In the Mahayana tradition we use the six paramitas, also known as the "six perfections" practice, to achieve complete enlightenment.

Q & A

Q: Lama, do the Theravadans have The Path of Seeing?

A: Yes. They have The Path of Seeing to see the selflessness of the person but not the selflessness of the phenomena. They have all of the five paths based on the thirty-seven enlightened factors.

Q: Can you explain the formless realm?

A: In the Buddhist cosmology there are three realms. We are currently living in the desire realm. All the humans and animals are all part of the desire realm. Actually the hungry ghosts, the beings in the hell realms, and even some of the titans and heavenly beings are still part of the desire realm.

Those beings who have good shamatha meditation can be reborn into the form realm. And then those beings who have done more shamatha practice and who have achieved even more realization can be reborn in the formless realm.

So the formless realm is where beings do not have a physical body. These beings have only four of the five aggregates. They do not have the first aggregate of "form" because one doesn't have the physical body in the formless realm. The formless beings are almost like spirits.

Here in the desire realm there are also spirits present, but they are not necessarily from the formless realm. The formless realm spirits are those who have cultivated more shamatha meditation. Those minds who have calmed all the emotions are born in the formless realm. So in Buddhism, the formless realm, and even most of the form realm, are considered to be the "heavenly realm" because beings there have much better shamatha meditation.

Q: Lama, do some beings take rebirth without passing through the bardo?

A: Yes, it is possible. It is said in the teachings that only two kinds of minds don't go through the bardo. Those who have lots of negative karma, like anger, may go directly to the hell realm. If someone has been very violent and has killed many people, and if that killer dies with a lot of anger, then he or she may go directly to the hell realm.

Or, on the other hand, those beings who have completely purified their negative karma may go directly to the Pure Land. But all other minds must go through the bardo after death. From the desire realm, if they are going to be reborn in the form or formless realms, they would still go through the bardo. But their bardo experience would resemble the realm they are about to take rebirth in.

Printed in Great Britain
by Amazon